VICTORIAN PERIODICALS

A Guide to Research

VICTORIAN PERIODICALS

A Guide to Research

Scott Bennett, Diana Dixon,

Mary Ruth Hiller, Lionel Madden,

John S. North, William H. Scheuerle,

Joanne Shattock, Rosemary T. VanArsdel,

J. Don Vann, Joel H. Wiener

Edited by

J. Don Vann and Rosemary T. VanArsdel

NEW YORK

The Modern Language Association of America

1978

Published by The Modern Language Association of America
62 Fifth Avenue, New York, New York 10011

Contents

Preface

The time is long past when it was necessary either to defend or to justify research and study of British Victorian periodicals. In the last fifteen years they have emerged as a major source of information for students of the nineteenth century. It is well recognized by scholars across the disciplines, in history, literature, economics, art history, social history, politics, the sciences, and many other fields, that periodicals offer a clear and very special window into the life and thought of the Victorian age. Because the field is so vast and unwieldy, the problem has instead become one of making proper use of periodicals while maintaining the greatest economy of the scholar's time. In the past, scholars have experienced extreme frustration working perhaps for weeks to solve a problem, only to stumble in the end over a source that would have taken them to the desired material in a matter of minutes. The purpose of the present volume is to aid in the solution of these problems. It is designed to assist researchers—be they undergraduates or graduate students, the idly curious or sophisticated scholars—who want to use Victorian periodicals but who do not know what the resources are.

The chapters have been arranged to address the chief problems encountered in using Victorian periodicals, and each is conceived of as an inquiry. What are the possibilities for the use of periodicals and approximately how many are there? What works will give a general history of the periodical press? How does one discover bibliographic material on periodicals? How does one find copies, or runs, of the desired periodical? How does one identify authors of articles published anonymously? What biographical aids are available to identify editors and contributors to periodicals? How does one assess the influence and importance of a periodical in its own time? And where can one find histories or studies of individual periodicals? Each of these questions is pertinent and necessary for the proper use of this valuable resource. The editors are aware of the duplication in this book of discussion of some of the major reference works, such as the *Dictionary of National Biography* and the *British Museum Catalogue of*

Printed Books. These seeming repetitions have been allowed to remain because we feel that each chapter should be a complete self-contained unit and because the various writers have discussed these reference works as research tools from differing standpoints.

The time frame for the studies is 1824–1900, selected primarily to parallel that employed by the *Wellesley Index.* Each chapter attempts to answer two questions: what are the basic resources in this field (including the strong and weak features of each) and how does the scholar use them? The term "periodical" is used in this book in its broadest sense so that it includes newspapers.

Those who have been at work in the periodical field over the last twenty or so years are convinced that study of untapped information in periodicals represents one of the great breakthroughs in modern Victorian scholarship. If the figure of sixteen thousand is accepted as the jumping-off point for the number of periodicals published in the Victorian era (and the work of the *Waterloo Directory* is rapidly revising that figure upward) one can see that within this framework may be found every conceivable variety of opinion, debate, political posturing, and social commentary. If one were able to select one year, say at mid-century, and sample from each of the sixteen thousand periodicals, what a kaleidoscopic glance into an era would be provided. While this is not presently feasible, with increasing adaptation of computer techniques to humanistic study, perhaps one day it may be possible to recapture "one year in the life of the nineteenth century."

As a result of interest in periodicals, many important events have occurred in the national and international scholarly world. First, and perhaps most important, in the late nineteen-fifties, Walter E. Houghton of Wellesley College launched his great *Wellesley Index to Victorian Periodicals* (discussed in detail in Chapter vii). Second, Michael Woolf, then at Indiana University (now at the University of Massachusetts, Amherst) began to prepare a "bibliography of Victorian journalism," which ultimately evolved into the *Waterloo Directory*, Phase i and ii, discussed in Chapter ii. When projects of this magnitude began to develop, the need for communication among scholars in the field became imperative. A new journal, the *Victorian Periodicals Newsletter*, was born in January 1968. In October 1969, a group of leading Victorian periodical specialists gathered in New York to found the international Research Society for Victorian Periodicals, with the appropriately Victorian acronymic title RSVP. The purpose of this group is to "encourage, assist, coordinate, and record the advancement of scholarly research in all areas pertaining to the newspaper, periodical, and other serial publications which appeared within the chronological compass of the Victorian age." The *Victorian Periodicals Newsletter* became the official organ of the Society. In 1976, a British branch of RSVP was established, the chief point of contact being the Victorian Studies Centre, at the University of Leicester.

What lies ahead in this field? The author or authors of each individual chapter have been asked to comment on desiderata in each area discussed, so that a brief scan will produce suggestions for future study. Certainly, increasing use of more sophisticated computer techniques will allow scholars to render the vastness of the material more manageable. Much has already been accomplished that ten years ago would have seemed impossible. Future research seems certain to add steadily and significantly to the knowledge of Victorian periodicals and, thus, of the Victorian world.

The editors would like to acknowledge the substantial support and encouragement they have received in this project from the officers and members of the Research Society for Victorian Periodicals, from the Victorian Division of the Modern Language Association, and from Walter S. Achtert, Director of Research Programs for the MLA. They would also like to acknowledge the support and encouragement, during trying times, of their respective spouses, Dolores and Paul.

J. Don Vann
Rosemary T. VanArsdel

Note: Throughout this book, the *Victorian Periodicals Newsletter* and *Victorian Studies* are abbreviated as *VPN* and *VS*, respectively.

VICTORIAN PERIODICALS

A Guide to Research

I

The Rationale— Why Read Victorian Periodicals?

John S. North
University of Waterloo

The great field for new discoveries is always the unclassified residuum. Round about the accredited and orderly facts of every science there ever flows a sort of dustcloud of exceptional observations, of occurrences minute and irregular and seldom met with, which it always proves more easy to ignore than to attend to.

William James

In answer to the question "Why read Victorian periodicals?" we need to be reminded of the reasons for reading old books at all. Every century has its own way of perceiving, so to escape the prejudices that characterize all born in this age we go back to an earlier day to look afresh on the world and, indeed, on ourselves. We also read old books to find out about our origins, to discover the purposes and methods of our forebears.

Periodical literature is the largest single source of Victorian material available to us, and the most comprehensive. If we retain the definition of a periodical generally used by library cataloguers, indexers, compilers, and editors—a publication of any frequency, from daily to annual, intended from the outset to be published at regular intervals without a pre-established termination date—we find that according to the most recent estimates the number of journals published in the years 1824 through 1900 exceeds fifty thousand. Although many of these journals had short life-spans, others ran for decades, some becoming centenarians. The number of issues, then, runs into the millions, and it is fair to say that every area of human activity is surveyed in the periodical press of Victorian Britain. Moreover, most of the commonly used sources of information about the age—the fiction, essays, handbooks, analyses, and reports—were first published in the periodicals. The novels of Thackeray, Trollope, and Eliot, the poetry of Tennyson and Arnold, and the essays of Carlyle, Huxley, and Ruskin are obvious examples. Others include the now-standard works on the history of the physical and social sciences and of government administration at all levels: the writings of John Tyndall, Walter Bagehot, William Gladstone. So if we are to adhere to that first dictum of literary, historical, and scientific study, that we must read the primary documents, then whatever our area of interest in the nineteenth century, we are obliged to read the periodicals.

The Victorian age is the first for which we have as sensitive a record of a civilization as the periodical press. Several developments account for its existence: an overwhelming rise in literacy, providing authors from an increasingly large part of society but also a broader reading public, including for the first time the lower-middle and poorer groups; the fascination of the public with newspaper and magazine reporting of rapid developments in technology and science and of the growth in empire and the flowering of the arts; the technological capacity of the press to satisfy the demand for inexpensive reading material literally overnight; and the development of communication systems, particularly the telegraph (Morse built his working model in 1835) and the steam engine, necessary for the collection of information and the dissemination of periodical issues. It is perhaps not fanciful to ascribe Britain's rise in the nineteenth century to the combination of its rapid increase in population, the appearance of several generations of people infused with the spirit of search, growth, and prosperity, and the nourishment of these generations by the periodical press, which encouraged the exchange of new ideas and techniques among the innovators and spread the practical results among the people. The periodical press began to act as a binding force in society, providing frequent and rapid communication among members of the many organizations that nourished Britain's growth and reminding the general public, through the daily newspapers, of the triumphs and challenges of empire.

The dominance of the periodical press in that day, unequalled in the twentieth century, provides still another reason Victorian students and scholars need read it: periodical literature was a fad. For example, within two decades the publishing firm of John Cassell developed from a single part-time press, operated in the evenings in his basement to produce labels for shilling packets of tea, to become one of the largest houses of industry in the realm, one based on the publication of religious and educational periodicals and serials. Another indicator is the number of periodicals started each year, which the *Times Tercentenary Handlist of English and Welsh Newspapers, Magazines and Reviews* (1920) places at 80 in 1824, 105 in 1844, 126 in 1864, and 276 in 1884. The periodicals had very little competition. Apart from the lecture platform the most serious competitor, both inexpensive and readily available, was liquor. But the temperance movement, supported massively by the Nonconformist churches, used first tea and then magazines, journals, serials, and newspapers to suppress the demon drink. So the periodical press became one of the chief entertainments of the people. Such it had not been before, and has not been since. We might object that twentieth-century newspaper and magazine circulation outnumbers that of the nineteenth, but when we consider the dramatic rise in population since 1900, proportion becomes an issue. More significantly, the twentieth century is the day of the publishing conglomerates, of the Beaverbrooks and Murdochs. The economics of mass production is now diminishing the number of small publications, thereby narrowing the range of reporting and variety of viewpoints. The periodical press has to some extent lost touch with the people, tending to proclaim the state of affairs as seen by an increasingly small and powerful group of journalists, propagandists, and politicians. It is less often the organ of public opinion, producing small local newspapers or magazines for a myriad of esoteric groups. Civilization may never again have so sensitive an instrument for registering its course as the Victorian periodical press.

There is a different reason for reading Victorian periodicals, one having nothing to do with our obligation as students and scholars and little to do with the prescriptions of scientific method and the rigors of the humanistic disciplines. Scrape away the dust from the yellowed pages of newspapers, crack open the stiff bindings of issues gathered together between fading boards, and we find ourselves more deeply immersed in the day than we could be by any other means. We find the photographs and etchings that convey the attitudes of the Victorians through the texture of their clothes and the expressions on their faces. We see the organization of their machinery, their transportation vehicles and systems, and their buildings. The imagination and aesthetic sense of each society whose *Proceedings* or *Report* or *Newsletter* we find—of the Pleasant Sunday Afternoon Society, Harleston Farmer's Club, or Thirsk Natural History Society—are conveyed through the page layouts and the advertisements, the trivia of event and plan. Often, if we are in pursuit of a particular topic or writer, it is the journals that provide incidental material more enlightening than the material we have been seeking. So the devotee of Gilbert and Sullivan may find the pages of *Musical Opinion and Music Trade Review* or *The Theatre; A Weekly Critical Review* rewarding in many details that have no direct bearing on the two partners. In the newspapers and journals we find material as it is selected and presented, not by our contemporaries, not by a few, not even by those who were great according to the judgment of their day or ours, but rather by many individuals, persons who are not professional journalists or, indeed, professionals of any kind. It is for the pleasure of browsing in an unfamiliar environment that we read the periodicals.

Periodicals and the Eminent

In 1825 Thomas Carlyle expressed shock at the triumph of journalism over literature. Yet in 1831, following unsuccessful attempts to sell *Sartor Resartus* in London, he turned to *Fraser's* to publish it serially; and throughout his career he was heavily dependent for publication on such periodicals as the *Foreign Review*, the *Foreign Quarterly Review*, the *Edinburgh Philosophical Journal*, *New Edinburgh Review*, *London Magazine*, the *Edinburgh Review*, and *Macmillan's Magazine*. It is common knowledge that most of the literary giants first gained esteem through the periodicals. Among those that come to mind are Dickens, who published *Sketches by Boz, Oliver Twist,* and *Hard Times* (to mention only a few) in serial parts in successive issues of magazines and who referred to himself as "a periodical essayist"; Arnold, who published *Culture and Anarchy* in the *Cornhill Magazine,* often wrote for *Pall Mall Gazette,* influenced the founders of the *Academy,* and contributed to such other journals as the *Educational Review, Macmillan's Magazine, Every Saturday, Eclectic Magazine,* and the *Nineteenth Century;* and Thackeray, who wrote and illustrated for many, including *Bentley's Magazine,* the *New Monthly, Punch,* the *Comic Almanac, Fraser's Magazine, Harper's Magazine,* the *Cornhill Magazine,* the *Quarterly Review, Corsair* (N.Y.) , the *National Standard,* and the *Foreign Quarterly Review.* Similar lists could be presented for Ruskin, Swinburne, Kingsley, Manning, and indeed for most of the eminent, not only among literary circles but also among scientists, theologians, and political figures. However, the implications of this knowledge—that most of the eminent depended greatly on periodicals—have not always been taken seriously. We must continue to go back to the periodical origins for textual studies, as John Butt and Kathleen Tillotson have done so ably in *Dickens at Work* (1957). Research on the context of those works that come to everyone's mind will always rely greatly on the periodicals that first published them. So, for instance, there is need for the study of the influence exerted on the serial novelists by events of the day and by the reviews, imitations, parodies, and dramatizations of their work, contemporary responses that appeared between the issues of a serial and, therefore, before the completion of the novel.

It is less well known that the eminent produced much that is not available outside the pages of old newspapers and magazines. Thackeray's first novel, *Catherine,* is not yet reliably reprinted from its original *Fraser's* version; nor is *The Luck of Barry Lyndon.* Apart from large works like these, much incidental journalism and magazine illustration awaits the researcher, material not yet identified, let alone analyzed.

Similarly, in the fine arts, a good collection of periodicals yields illustrations of Doré or Cruikshank. Browsing through family journals, such as the *Sunday at Home,* we find references to the leaders of the empire (the Gladstones and the Disraelis), the eminent scientists (the W. B. Carpenters and the Charles Pritchards), and leaders in other fields. Yet this material has not been collected, generally speaking, for until recently it has been inaccessible. One gauge of the work still to be done in Victorian studies is the fact that there are no adequate biographies, bibliographies, or even collected editions for fully eighty percent of the sixty-two members of the Metaphysical Society, a group representing the elite in every area—medicine, law, education, natural science, moral science, literature, politics, fine arts, mathematics, and the church—that met eight times yearly from 1869 through 1880. One of the reasons for this neglect is that most of their work appeared in periodical literature, and many of those periodicals are difficult to identify and obtain.

Not only did the eminent Victorians make their individual voices heard through the periodicals, they developed whole choirs, as it were, by becoming editors. As if taking the cue of S. T. Coleridge, who had edited the *Friend*, Dickens edited *Household Words*; J. S. Mill, the *London Review*, later the *London and Westminster Review* (George Eliot was to be the assistant editor, 1851–53, when it was *Westminster Review*); and Newman, the *British Critic* (his *Apologia pro Vita Sua* was prompted by Kingsley's attack in *Macmillan's Magazine*). Thackeray was proprietor of the *National Standard* in 1833 and editor of the *Cornhill* in 1860; Walter Bagehot, editor of the *Economist*; Sir George Grove, of *Macmillan's Magazine*; R. H. Hutton, of the *Spectator*; James Knowles, of the *Contemporary Review* and the *Nineteenth Century*; John Morley, of the *Fortnightly Review*; Leslie Stephen, of the *Cornhill Magazine*; J. A. Froude, of *Fraser's Magazine*. Such a list has no end, but the point needs to be made clearly: a study of the thought and influence of these people should take into account their work as editors, the articles they solicited or accepted, the policies they developed, the incidental material that caught their attention, the reviews and articles they often wrote to provide extra copy to flesh out an issue.

Although much research remains to be done on the eminent literary people, there is even more that needs to be known about those whose names are a little less familiar, not because they contributed less to the Victorian age, but because their contributions were in fields other than the arts and humanities—in the sciences, technology and engineering, the church, and government—and thus quickly became dated. A few examples are of interest. Sir John Charles Bucknill made perhaps the greatest contribution of the nineteenth century to the enlightenment of the public toward the insane, the improvement of asylum care, and the reform of legislation with regard to the criminally insane; he was the first to oppose successfully the use of mechanical restraints for the insane and profit-making asylums, and the first to institute out-patient care and to make a psychological study of alcoholism. To discover more about this man we need to turn to the pages of the journal he founded, the *Asylum Journal of Mental Science,* later known as the *British Journal of Psychiatry.* A similar instance is that of G. D. Campbell, the Duke of Argyll, who was Chancellor of St. Andrews, Lord Rector of Glasgow University, Postmaster General, President of the Royal Society of Edinburgh, Secretary of State for India, and, at the height of the empire, one of the greatest contributors to British foreign policy in Ireland, India, and Egypt. This statesman, like most Victorians, wrote prolifically in the journals of education, science, and religion, but only a negligible amount of his work has been collected. The pages of the *Wellesley Index* provide us with the beginnings of a list of his periodical writings. Henry Alford, Dean of Canterbury, is best known for his annotated Greek New Testament, soon translated into English; in it he accepted the superiority of the German critics, and the work marked a new epoch in biblical studies in England. He had been a member of the Cambridge Apostles and later became renowned for his preaching, as well as for his willingness to recognize Nonconformist ministers and for advocating voluntarism regarding church and state. But it is difficult to find adequate information on the mind and personality and accomplishments of Alford without recourse to *Dearden's Miscellany,* which he edited, and the *Contemporary Review,* of which he was the founding editor. It is persons like Bucknill, Campbell, and Alford who, because they did not write literary classics, have faded somewhat from our view a hundred years later. Nevertheless, they are at least as important as the novelists, essayists, and poets in any measure of the contributions of Victorian Britain to Western and indeed world civilization. To rediscover them we must have the periodicals.

Major Movements

Historians have rarely treated religious journalism as a subject, and never systematically, points out R. D. Altick in *Victorian People and Ideas* (1973). Yet religion has been given as much attention as any of the areas in Victorian historiography. One explanation is that the great bulk of religious journalism was produced by the Nonconformists, while the Anglo-Catholic movement, upon which our attention has been concentrated, relied more on the bound volume. Another reason is that the Nonconformists concentrated on the lower-middle and poorer classes, especially on the alcoholics, for whom they prepared temperance journals, and the newly literate, for whom they prepared histories, religious fiction, serialized formats of the Bible, and general information magazines. This kind of material does not have much appeal for the twentieth-century academic, who is often, to use Schleiermacher's phrase, among "the cultured despisers of religion." We cannot find in that kind of journal the succinct, carefully reasoned eloquence of the Anglo-Catholic movement. We disapprove of the religious enthusiasm that characterized the Nonconformists, and quietly demur when people such as W. O. G. Lofts and D. J. Adley, in *The Men behind Boys' Fiction* (1970), say:

> I would love to see some advanced evangelist, uncorrupted by airy-fairy theory, start out from the bald fact that my generation, raised on this kind of reading, produced an infinitely smaller percentage of juvenile delinquency and layabouts than the brood which is currently supposed to be raised on today's approved wishy-washy pabulum.

So we ignore the religious journalism. Although we have been told by John Gay, in *The Geography of Religion in England* (1971), that by the 1850s Nonconformists outnumbered Roman Catholics ten to one, we continue to pour our efforts into Newman studies. This is not to question the value of Newman, but it is to make a judgment on our sense of balance, our perspective. To be fair, of course, one must add that the periodicals in which the voice of the Nonconformists was heard throughout the British Isles have not been readily available. But this is not an adequate reason. We need research on the periodicals that will parallel Valentine Cunningham's *Everywhere Spoken Against: Dissent in the Victorian Novel* (1975) and that will consider the influential Nonconformist journals in their own right. One way in which pertinent titles can now be discovered is to browse through the pages of the recent *Waterloo Directory of Victorian Periodicals, 1824–1900; Phase I* (1976), by Wolff, North, and Deering, looking in the alphabetized listing for entries under the headings Baptist, Congregationalist, Methodist, Presbyterian, Salvation Army, Society of Friends, and Unitarian or for listings of interdenominational societies. Sometimes the Nonconformist journals can best be tracked down through a single leading figure, such as John Cassell, who began a periodical publishing house in 1848 and within four years was publishing the *Teetotal Times*, the *Standard* ("to the friends of Religious, Political and Commercial Freedom throughout the world —to all who are opposed to Intolerance, the Gibbet, Intemperance, War, and all other systems which degrade, demoralize, brutalize and destroy mankind"), the *Working Man's Friend and Family Instructor*, the *Freeholder, Pathway, John Cassell's Library* (monthly), and *Popular Educator*. It was Cassell who brought Doré to fame in Britain by commissioning him to illustrate the serialized format of the Bible. Another remarkable Nonconformist was John Edward Taylor, editor of the *Manchester Guardian* and son of its founder. He made the paper a daily, then cut its price by half. In 1868 he acquired the *Manchester Evening News*. A staunch supporter of the Unitarian Manchester College, the British and Foreign Bible Society, and the Manchester Educational Aid Society, Taylor was instrumental in the formation, in 1868, of the Press Association, which gained a footing in the House of Commons, freeing the provincial papers from the inadequate and often inaccurate reporting of news agencies. Although neither Taylor's two newspapers nor all Cassell's periodicals were religious, we cannot pretend to understand the content and influence of these publications without considering the motives of their editors.

Pursuing the periodical publications of the Nonconformists, "The Other Victorian Christians," to use the phrase of Peter Marsh (*VS*, 1972), we are rapidly led into two other movements of the day: children's literature and missions. Both are much neglected; both present questions for which only periodicals provide answers.

The Nonconformists dominated the field of children's literature, producing Sunday school papers, boys' and girls' magazines, and chap books. Curiously, Great Britain in the nineteenth century was the first nation in the world to engage in massive publication of children's literature, and, not surprisingly, it is still a leader in that field. Not all the Nonconformist children's literature was explicitly Christian. George Andrew Hutchinson was the founding editor of *Boy's Own Paper*, and he took care not to make it a religious paper, although he himself was deeply religious and founded a church in a London suburb. He encouraged A. N. Malan, among the most prolific and popular of the magazine's writers, to produce about thirty serialized novels. Hutchinson also edited *Toilers of the Deep*, a mission magazine, and the *Sunday School World*. We need research that will answer the following questions about Victorian children's literature: What was the proportion of children's magazines written by the Nonconformists, and what proportion of Victorian children's literature appeared in the periodicals? To what extent were the periodicals narrowly sectarian, and how much did they contribute to the formation of a national spirit or to general information and education? Can it be said of the Nonconformist writers for children, as Ian Bradley has said of the Evangelicals in general, in *The Call to Seriousness: The Evangelical Impact on the Victorians* (1976), that they were responsible for the coming of an incorruptible professional civil service and for a growing concern for education of the poor?

The Nonconformists were not the only Victorian Christians writing children's literature. George Macdonald, editor of *Good Words for the Young* (1869–77), was also writing, as were Charlotte Yonge, editor of the *Monthly Packet*, Edward Lear, Lewis Carroll, Kenneth Grahame, and John Ruskin. Of course, much of the work has deservedly fallen by the wayside: we do not now claim outstanding artistic merit for Mrs. Molesworth, Mrs. Ewing, or Mrs. Gatty. Just the same, we do need to inquire into the influence of the Victorian Christians on the development of form and content in children's literature. Why did they believe children to be worth so much attention? Is the tone of the best British children's literature—so remarkably free from condescension, so holistic, even sacramental in its world view—in part due to the attitudes and beliefs of these early writers? In answering such questions we will be obliged to turn the pages of the old children's magazines, and suspend for the moment our belief that twentieth-century standards alone are valid: if the greater part of Victorian children's literature was as bad as our literary historians tell us, why was it so popular at the time? Perhaps A. A. Milne's observation about Kenneth Grahame applies to others as well: "But I must give you a word of warning. When you sit down to it, don't be so ridiculous as to suppose that you are sitting in judgment—on the art of Kenneth Grahame. You are merely sitting in judgment on yourself— it is you who are on trial."

The impact of missions, both home and foreign, is another much-neglected area of Victorian studies and one for which periodicals are an enormous, unopened mine. The history of missions is neglected, no doubt, for the same reasons that Nonconformism is. When the church is studied, it is usually studied in the context of theological debate rather than of its impact on the slum areas, the educational system, the development of the empire. As we hear ringing in our ears Arnold's scathing phrase, "hole-and-corner religion," so too we see *Punch* cartoons with an ethereal young British woman in Roman helm, toga, and sandals looking across the sea to a shadowy group of dark-skinned starving children, while in the foreground a "little London Arab" on the embankment begs, "Please'm, ain't we black enough to be cared for?" Or we remember the "telescopic philanthropy" of Dickens' Mrs. Jellyby, who, while her own neglected brood batter themselves around her dirty household, busies herself about the welfare of the natives of Borrioboola-Gha, on the left bank of the Niger. But these caricatures of the Nonconformists and missions are surely no more than that. It is time that we asked ourselves how much of the social reform at home—the kind of reform that warded off the bloody revolutions sweeping the rest of Europe—was accomplished by the mission societies, many of which still exist, to be remarked upon by visitors to Great Britain. We need to inform ourselves by reading the quarterly reports and newsletters of societies such as the Society for the Study and Care of Inebriety, the Society for the Promotion of Female Education in China, Africa, and the East, the

Society for the Extinction of the Slave Trade, the Patagonian Missionary Society, the Society for Superseding the Necessity of Climbing Boys, the Society for Promoting the Education of the Poor in Ireland, the China Inland Mission, the Society for Educating the Poor in Newfoundland, the Society for Organizing Charitable Relief, and the British and Foreign Sailors' Society. These titles seem quaint a century later, when the state has taken up such causes. Yet their quaintness and humorousness and our reticence about piety and do-goodism should not keep us from a hardheaded assessment of the contribution of these groups, who, after all, represent a very large segment of Victorian life. To read through the pages of Henry Mayhew's *London Labour and the London Poor* (1861) is to find a startling example of that same spirit that prompted the Victorian mission societies—the same tone, the same language, the same commitment, the same fund of pity. As we look back through the periodical reports of the societies, we find that many of them, though not explicitly evangelical or even religious in their purpose or their charter, were in fact the product of the self-conscious Christian temper of their founders.

In the *Sunday at Home* for 1888 we find a report of Sir Arthur Peel's address to the annual conference of the British and Foreign Bible Society. Peel, speaker of the House of Commons, pointed out that by the year of the Jubilee, 1887, Victoria's subjects had grown from 130 million in 1837 to 300 million, British territory had increased from two million to eight million square miles, and the United Kingdom alone had increased ten million in population. Then he underscored the belief that he shared with the Society, that Britain had a responsibility far beyond her financial one. A note several lines down provides a report of the Society's progress in promoting the writing of Braille books and sheets by sighted people, on a voluntary basis. It is this kind of information that the periodicals provide in abundance for those who care to take seriously the role of missions. It may well be shown that the energy of the periodical publishers and writers, these "hole-and-corner" Nonconformists, was not in fact expended on defending sectarian identities, that their highly charged Hebraism did not hinder their Hellenizing spirit, and that their breadth of interest, generosity of spirit, and intellectual acumen were astonishing. Desmond Bowen, in *The Idea of the Victorian Church* (1968), points out that the role of missions has been documented, yet to judge by the content of university classes, or published research, or invited papers read to learned societies, we have not responded to the documentation: it has not had much of an impact on us. Perhaps as the work of the Research Society for Victorian Periodicals proceeds in the next decade and as the journals, magazines, and newspapers of the day become more readily identified and available, we will discover not only the extent to which the missions permeated Britain and her empire but also the motives and results of that influence. Perhaps we will be able to articulate some credible alternatives to the Marxian theory of empire.

David DeLaura reminds us in *Victorian Prose: A Guide to Research* (1973) that much of the best prose is some variety of journalism or reviewing. This best prose includes the social and political history of the age. The argument for the use of periodicals in our study of social and political movements is the same as that for the use of the periodicals in other areas: the best-known writers first appeared in the periodicals; much of what they wrote has not yet been collected but is available in the old magazine files tucked away on the shelves of British libraries; and much ungathered material by lesser names, as well as casual reportage on the names and events that made social and political history, is available in these same files. An example is that of Walter Bagehot, editor of the *Economist* and the *National Review*, who first published much of his material on political economy, the history of parliament, and literature and biography in the magazines. Even when we have the complete collected works being edited by Norman St. John-Stevas, we will need to return to the pages of the *Fortnightly Review*, the *Economist*, and the *Popular Science Monthly* to discover the context of his writings and the popular response to them. The same is true of J. A. Froude, for whom we have no collected edition. While editing *Fraser's Magazine* he wrote extensively for other journals, particularly the *Westminster Review*. One of the several unhappy incidents in his life was his visit in 1874 to South Africa, where he was sent by the Earl of Carnarvon, secretary of state for the colonies, to find means of overcoming the barriers to confederation of the various states. He took the part of South Africa, effectively ruined the hopes of his friend Carnarvon to establish a federation, and caused considerable stir in Africa and at home. In order to learn the details of this incident and to understand the early history of this country, which now is a major factor in international stability, it is necessary to obtain not only a copy of his report, published as a parliamentary paper in 1876, but also his defense of his position in the *Quarterly Review* (1877), Lord Blachford's reply in the *Edinburgh Review* a few months later, and Froude's rejoinder of February 1879 in the *Quarterly Review*. Yet the dust Froude raised on this occasion was little compared to the public reaction to his *History of England* (1856–70) and his biography of Thomas Carlyle (1881–84). No balanced judgment of these works can be made without recourse to the reviews that flurried around them.

If we approach Victorian political and social history through particular events rather than through a single figure, we find ourselves even more dependent upon the journalism. One of the last barriers to fall in the attack on Victorian periodicals will be that of subject indexing, although works such as *Poole's Index to Periodical Literature, 1802–1881* (with supplements to 1906), W. R. Le-Fanu's *British Periodicals of Medicine* (1938), Helene Roberts' *British Art Periodicals of the Eighteenth and Nineteenth Centuries* (1974), and E. C. Richardson's *Periodical Articles on Religion* (1890–99) have begun the attack. For now, we must rely on the uncertain yet fruitful method of browsing through the listings arranged chronologically, as is the *Times Tercentenary Handlist of English and Welsh Newspapers, Magazines and Reviews*; by title and author of specific articles, as is the *Wellesley Index to Victorian Periodicals*; or alphabetically by title, as is the *Waterloo Directory of Victorian Periodicals*. The forthcoming Subject Guide to the *Waterloo Directory* will be the first comprehensive general subject guide to periodical titles. But whether it be the Irish famine of the 1840s, socialist trade unionism, H. M. Stanley's search for Livingstone, or the growth of public education that interests us, the newspapers will seldom fail to provide a range of opinion and extent of detail available nowhere else. It is true that twentieth-century critics and historians have provided valuable assessments of many Victorian movements and occasions, yet they have the bias of their age, their partisanships, their private motives. Finally, we must fall back to the periodicals as the documents closest to the time and personalities involved. The diversity of opinions of the editors and their contributors provides the breadth of perspective that often crucially affects our understanding of events. We might, for example, find differing reviews of a single Victorian book, such as J. R. Seeley's *Ecce Homo* (1866), or news reports in both a provincial and a London paper about another cholera outbreak, or an essay in which T. H. Huxley compares the Salvation Army to the Franciscans (as he does in the *Pall Mall Gazette*) as a supplement to reviews of William Booth's *In Darkest England* (1890) and of G. B. Shaw's *Major Barbara* (1907). Again and again, our source is the periodicals.

One of the deepest influences on the twentieth century has been that of the social sciences. They are invoked to heal our illnesses, to justify our government procedures, to relieve us of our sins, to popularize our religion, to cement foreign relations, to raise our children, to inspire our employees. The idea of progress is as entrenched in the disciplines of psychology, sociology, and anthropology as it is in the natural sciences, a fact to which the hierarchical ranking of publications by date attests. Yet remarkably little attention is paid to the rise of these disciplines in the nineteenth century. Consideration is given to the very few acknowledged masters (Cornell University Press is preparing a concordance to the works of Freud), but little attention is paid to people like John Lubbock and James Sully, who contributed greatly to the development of the social sciences through their work as editors, their articles, and their addresses to learned and popular audiences. If we ever entertain the notion that a wrong turn might have been taken in the study of sociology, anthropology, or psychology, that a serious lapse might have occurred or a crucial idea been neglected, we must look back to their beginnings and trace the lives and writings of the earliest leaders.

John Lubbock was one of the fathers of sociology. A banker, member of the House of Commons and then the House of Lords, and an amateur scientist in a day when amateur scientists still had credibility, he pursued anthropology when few others did. He was an intimate of Darwin and Huxley, extending their work by writing *Prehistoric Times* (1859), *The Origin of Civilization and the Primitive Condition of Man* (1870), and *Marriage, Totems and Religion* (1911), which were translated into many languages and went through several reprintings. His contribution to anthropology cannot be measured adequately by a study of his printed volumes, however, for he was a frequent speaker at meetings of the Royal Society and at working men's organizations, ranking close to Huxley as a popularizer of Darwin. His presidential addresses to the many scientific associations on which he served have yet to be collected from among the annals of those groups; the same is true of his speeches that appeared in the *American Journal of Science, Popular Science*, the *New Review, Working Men's College Journal*, the *Nineteenth Century*, and *Strand*. James Sully contributed as much in the field of psychology as Lubbock did in anthropology. A study of his books, *Sensation and Intuition* (1874), *Illusions* (1881), *Children's Ways* (1897), and *An Essay on Laughter* (1902), should be supplemented by a reading of his many essays on humor, dreams, child psychology, and educational psychology in order to enlarge our historical perspective of those important areas of contemporary study. Those essays are only available in the periodicals.

Lesser Names and Movements

Since the appearance of the *Wellesley Index* there can be no controversy about the value of the major periodicals. But what about the thousands of obscure titles? Might it not be true, as one reviewer of the *Waterloo Directory* has suggested, that expensive efforts to discover and catalogue the more than fifty thousand titles we know to have been published will prove only that there were many titles? Can such unknowns as *Country Gentleman's Almanac*, or the *Irish Reader*, or *Notes of Observations of Injurious Insects* offer enough to make worthwhile their identification, let alone a patient reading? Surely the many ephemeral titles such as *Notes to the People* and *Norton Chronicle*, ones that lasted for only a few issues, can contribute little to our understanding of the period. Why not limit ourselves to, say, five hundred titles that we can gain control of as thoroughly as Houghton has of the *Wellesley Index* titles?

Yet, on reflection, we must admit that we can never trust our present evaluation of what is and what is not significant. These opinions are always subject to fashion, to personal prejudice, to the limitations of our knowledge. We cannot see the value of the unfamiliar, and, until we have these unknown titles under bibliographical control, we can hardly dismiss their value. Although the information in the *Wellesley Index* that pertains to familiar names and movements is of great immediate interest, other information is valuable because it lightens hitherto dark, unknown areas.

What are the rewards of a close study of the more obscure journals? There we can often find a fact that in itself seems trivial, but that adds a piece to a larger puzzle. The small-circulation, highly specialized journals and magazines often print obituaries. Knowing that Edmund Gosse's father, Philip, a naturalist and painter, was a prominent member of several scientific societies, we might discover something about both men by reading the elder Gosse's obituaries in the publications of the societies to which he belonged. That information, in turn, might alter our perspective on Edmund's devastating book *Father and Son* (1907), in which the rancorous tone leaves us ill at ease with the son's judgments.

Another method of using the obscure journals to discover information about lesser names and movements is what might be termed the "geographical method." That is, once a date and a place have been isolated, a great deal of material may be found by determining all the periodicals published in that place at that time. The recent eight-volume *British Library Catalogue of the Newspaper Library, Colindale* (1975) is useful. It divides into two parts: volumes one through four list newspapers, magazines, and journals alphabetically by place of publication; volumes five through eight repeat the entries of the first four, but alphabetically by title. The *British Bibliography of Newspapers*, presently being published county by county under the direction of C. A. Toase, is also useful. More information about the publications in any county can be found in the Victoria County Histories series, which consists of several large volumes per county. For a number of the counties, such as Wiltshire, a brief history of the major publications, including type of coverage and bias, is recorded. The Subject Guide to the *Waterloo Directory* will be a useful supplement to these sources, for it will contain a list of titles by place of publication as well as by subject, including many titles not in the Colindale collection. So if we want information on the Birmingham Festival of 1846, in which Haydn's *Creation*, Mendelssohn's *Elijah* (composed for the occasion), Handel's *Messiah*, and Beethoven's *Missa Solemnis* were performed on four successive evenings, we should use the above sources to determine all Birmingham publications at the time. These might provide information about the festival not only from the music historian's perspective, but also from that of the various wings of the church and the popular press. We could expect to find details about the performers, composers, sponsors, and even other musical compositions and performances leading up to or resulting from this festival.

Needless to say, much trivia will inevitably be uncovered in the files of obscure periodicals. In passing through the listings of titles, searching for a single magazine, the student will certainly be oppressed by irrelevant material. When the laborious task of turning page after page of hundreds of issues is begun, the patience of even the most single-minded scholar will be tried as the dust accumulates on hands, face, and clothing. However, the trivia that must be passed through and put aside, even that which offers up not a single useful or interesting detail, will still provide a certain sense of the Victorian era. That society, no less than our own, reveals itself in its pettiest details.

II

The Bibliographic Control of Victorian Periodicals

Scott Bennett
University of Illinois Library at Urbana-Champaign

This *Guide* and the scholarship it seeks to serve exist because nineteenth-century Britain was a "journalizing society." It adopted periodicals as the chief means of carrying forward the discourse by which a society comes to know itself. And because the technology of communication developed as it did, the nineteenth century was the only period in which the written word dominated mass communication. The modern world remains a "journalizing" one, but the technologies for this activity have multiplied. In sharp contrast, the Victorian era is unique in its dependence on print and on periodical publication. How ironic, then, that the very periodicals that gave the era its individuality rapidly lost their usefulness even to contemporary readers because there was no way to know what was in them: they were under inadequate bibliographic control. The inability to get to much of the seminal writing of the period marks a radical failure in the age's communication with itself, and the second half of the century saw a burgeoning effort to provide better access to periodical literature. It was no empty boast that the militant liberal R. R. Bowker made to a meeting of British librarians in 1882, when he said "it will be a chief glory of the nineteenth century, that it has organized knowledge."

This chapter sets out the means developed since about 1850 for bringing periodicals under bibliographic control. It has two major sections that reflect the history of periodical discourse itself. The first of these sections is concerned with the effort simply to inventory titles, to list or catalogue the periodicals that exist; the second section is concerned with the effort to make the individual contents of periodicals available to readers. Following these major sections is a short third one, which lists a few essays similar in scope to this one and a few other valuable works in related areas. This last section also presents some comments on important work under way (as of January 1977) and on bibliographic work that still needs to be done.

The Bibliographic Control of Periodical Titles: Inventories

Library catalogues were the first inventories of periodicals in the English-speaking world; they were followed by a number of trade publications that appeared in the nineteenth century and, later, by a variety of retrospective lists that most often addressed regional or special subjects.

LIBRARY CATALOGUES

The volumes on library shelves (but not the content of these volumes) pose the first problem of bibliographic control. Students of periodicals will often find individual library catalogues useful in identifying elusive journals. Catalogues of regionally important libraries, such as (1) Andrea Crestadoro's *Catalogue of the Books in the Manchester Free Library* (1864), or the catalogues of special libraries or institutes are especially important. The (2) *Standortskatalog wichtiger Zeitungbestände in deutschen Bibliotheken* published by the Deutsches Institut für Zeitungskunde (Leipzig: Hiersemann, 1933) exemplifies this second kind of catalogue and the utility of searching in what might at first seem an out-of-the-way collection. For here, among a not particularly distinguished inventory of English-language papers, is a list of German-language newspapers that were published in Great Britain—an easy means of identifying this particular bibliographic group. In what follows, no attempt is made to list regional library catalogues, but a few of the most important research library or institute catalogues are described.

The great (3) *General Catalogue of Printed Books* issued by the British Museum (1965–) is by far the most useful of the library catalogues. Those familiar with American catalogues, in which periodicals are entered by title, will have to remember that the British Museum catalogue was compiled under rules inspired by Anthony Panizzi, Britain's greatest nineteenth-century librarian, who was himself influenced by the eighteenth-century practice of cataloguing periodicals together, as a group, rather than separately, under their titles. Well, almost together. Periodicals are inventoried in the British Museum catalogue under two collective devices: under "Periodical Publications," a form heading in Volumes 184–86 that is subdivided by place of publication (e.g., Brighton, Edinburgh, London), and under a form heading made up of a place name and the name of the issuing body— normally an academy, society, museum, or some other corporate body. Happily, the British Museum catalogue provides cross-references between the title entry for each periodical and these form-heading entries where full bibliographic information is located, so even a title search will be fruitful—eventually. Users should be cautioned not to confuse the entries for London that fill one of the volumes devoted to "Periodical Publications" with those that fill three other volumes under "London" as a place name. Great numbers of periodicals are listed in both places. Newspapers are not inventoried at all in the *Catalogue*; they appear in a supplementary British Museum catalogue of (4) *Newspapers Published in Great Britain and Ireland, 1801–1900* (1905). Here individual titles are arranged by place of publication.

A few other library catalogues merit attention because of the distinction of the collections they inventory or because they were seminal works in the bibliographic control of periodical literature in their respective fields. Periodical publication came into being in response to the communication needs of the natural sciences, and the sciences were the earliest and best-served fields bibliographically. Among library catalogues, (5) Samuel H. Scudders' *Catalogue of Scientific Serials of All Countries including the Transactions of Learned Societies in the Natural Sciences and Mathematical Sciences, 1633–1876* (1879; rpt. 1965) was a pioneering and influential work. It contains about 550 British titles in the pure sciences, but none in medicine, pharmacy, agriculture, technology, and engineering. Henry Carrington Bolton extended bibliographic control to a much wider range of the applied sciences in his (6) *Catalogue of Scientific and Technical Periodicals* (1885; 2nd ed., 1897). Medical periodicals are not included here either, but coverage does extend to nearly the end of the century. Some 8,600 titles of all nations and languages are listed, but there is no access to them by nationality or place of publication. Another important catalogue, not tied to a specific library, is the (7) *International Catalogue of Scientific Literature: List of Journals* (1903). This is a list of then-current periodicals that the International Council meant to index; it includes about 470 titles published in the United Kingdom. Finally, there is the (8) *Catalogue of the Periodical Publications in the Library of the Royal Society of London* (1912); it supercedes an earlier catalogue (1881) and includes a great many serial titles published by government departments, universities and colleges, and other public bodies, as well as the more usual periodicals.

Library catalogues inventory the holdings only of the given library at a given time and so never approach bibliographic "completeness." Union lists inventory the holdings of several libraries, regionally or even nationally. But as important as these union lists are for bibliographic purposes, they are designed first of all to provide access to periodicals. For that reason they are not discussed here, but in Chapter iii of this *Guide*. The two union lists of greatest bibliographic importance are the national ones, the pioneer American (9) *Union List of Serials* (3rd ed., 1965) and the (10) *British Union Catalogue of Periodicals* (1955–). (11) William S. Ward's *Index and Finding List of Serials Published in the British Isles 1789–1832* (1953) includes many titles not found in the *Union List of Serials* or *British Union Catalogue of Periodicals*.

TRADE PUBLICATIONS

Contemporary trade publications, like library catalogues and union lists, have limits of usefulness that are sharply defined by the often nonbibliographic purposes they are designed to serve.

Trade publications, compiled annually as guides for booksellers or for purchasers of advertising space in newspapers and periodicals, report much commercial information but do not always provide the range of bibliographic information that a catalogue or union list will. These trade publications are sometimes hard to locate in library collections because they were thought to have no lasting reference value. But they are a treasure trove of information about periodicals. Trade publications therefore warrant special attention even though relatively few scholars, at least in North America, will find good runs of these nineteenth-century publications in their libraries.

Bookdealers always need to know what books are available for sale, from whom, and at what price. Book fairs and booksellers' catalogues are the oldest devices for managing this information; in a journalizing society a book-trade journal was an obvious expedient. In 1837, Sampson Low began issuing (12) the *Publishers' Circular*, a twice-monthly journal announcing new publications and reporting a considerable amount of miscellaneous literary and book-trade news. The annual classified indexes to the early years give access to some periodical titles under the entries "Magazines, reviews, &c." (1837–38) and "Annual pictorial publications and miscellaneous periodicals" (1843–45).

The *Publishers' Circular* was far from complete in listing periodicals, and after 1845 gave no separate access to them. This difficulty was remedied in 1847 with the publication of a new annual, (13) the *London Catalogue of Periodicals, Newspapers and Transactions of Societies Also a List of Metropolitan Printing Societies and Clubs* (1847–85). Here monthlies, quarterlies, "transactions," and "Newspapers, Weekly Publications, etc." are listed separately, with the price and the publication address for each. A separate list describes subscription societies (e.g., the Camden Society, the Archaeological Institute).

Both the *Publishers' Circular* and the *London Catalogue of Periodicals* addressed people who made their living buying and selling books. As advertising established itself as the economic basis of periodical publication, a new species of trade publication appeared—the advertiser's guide. The best and most informative of these began just a year earlier than the *London Catalogue of Periodicals*: it was (14) Charles Mitchell's *Newspaper Press Di-*

rectory and Advertisers' Guide (1846–1907). *Mitchell's*, as it is known, soon became the authoritative press guide, and in 1861 the Post Office adopted it as its official identification of London and provincial papers. Fortunately, Microcard Editions has reissued *Mitchell's* on microfilm (1968). In addition to a host of miscellaneous but informative essays on the history and the profession of journalism, each year's edition of *Mitchell's* listed every journal known to be published in England, Wales, Scotland, the Channel Islands, and the Isle of Man, with a rich account of each title—its price, frequency of publication, date of establishment, political affiliation and principal interests, proprietors and publishers, and even the population and commercial profile of the area served. In 1879, a particularly useful index to various classes of newspapers (e.g., agriculture, civil service, photography) began to appear, and after 1885 a supplement included colonial newspapers. Continental papers were first listed in 1878; American newspapers, in 1880. *Mitchell's* offers a wealth of information about periodicals, but is difficult to use because its design and contents changed from time to time during the century. An invaluable guide to the riches in *Mitchell's* is Susan Gliserman's "*Mitchell's Newspaper Press Directory*: 1846–1907" (*VPN*, 1969).

Mitchell's was the best of many contemporary newspaper directories. The *New Cambridge Bibliography of English Literature* (1969, III, 1787) lists several other advertising agents' guides. After *Mitchell's*, the best and longest-lived of these guides is (15) *May's British and Irish Press Guide, and Advertiser's Handbook & Dictionary* (1874–), continued since 1890 as (16) *Willing's Press Guide and Advertisers' Directory and Handbook*. Similar in most respects to *Mitchell's*, *May's* does include a valuable tabular presentation of some bibliographic information and political coloration of the periodicals, and it lists magazines separately from newspapers. The "Dictionary" of the title is an index of various special interests, professions, trades, religious denominations, and the like, along with the periodicals addressed to them.

RETROSPECTIVE LISTS: GENERAL

A few librarians and those persons serving the needs of the book trade worked in the nineteenth century to bring under bibliographic control the great flood of periodicals that characterizes the age. Everything else that we have was prepared after the fact, as so often happens in bibliography, and thus suffers from the difficulties of a retrospective effort to collect information about an essentially transient phenomenon. These retrospective lists were developed in response to perceived needs; their history has no internal logic but derives from developments in scholarship generally. These retrospective lists are presented here in three categories: those that address the problem of listing all periodicals, those that list the periodicals of specific regions, and those that are concerned with periodicals in special subject fields.

The first retrospective list of general periodicals appeared as Appendix C, pages 903–05, of (17) the *English Catalogue of Books, 1835–1863* (1864). Other volumes of the *English Catalogue of Books* published during the nineteenth century contained no such list. Superseding this incomplete list is the great (18) *Times Tercentenary Handlist of English and Welsh Newspapers, Magazines and Reviews* (1920). J. G. Muddiman compiled the *Handlist,* working with the collections at the British Museum and the Bodleian Library. He excluded Irish and Scottish publications, annuals and year books, periodicals published by learned institutions and societies, and local church magazines; the entries are brief, with some information on editors and successive titles. Within these exclusions and limitations Muddiman claimed the *Handlist* was "practically exhaustive" for the seventeenth and nineteenth centuries. This is always a dangerous claim to make, and bibliographers knew from the first that the *Handlist* did not fulfill it. A number of articles appearing in *Notes and Queries* during 1921 and 1922 provide information on titles not included in the *Handlist* and suggest that the dependence on only two libraries in London and Oxford resulted in a serious neglect of the provincial press. One writer, "M." (*N&Q,* 1921), reports that a preliminary search of the *Handlist* shows it to lack at least 150 titles published in one county alone. Its shortcomings notwithstanding, the *Handlist* is an impressive and bibliographically groundbreaking work; it has become a standard—and probably the most widely known—reference work of its kind.

A book that should be better known among students of periodicals is (19) the *List of the Serial Publications of Foreign*

Governments 1815–1931 (comp. Winifred Gregory, 1932). Governments were no less active publishers of periodicals than were other special-interest groups, though their publications are often thought of as "documents" rather than as periodicals. The material is serial in nature, however, and probably had as much or more consequence for many trades, professions, and other groups as did their acknowledged periodicals. Gregory lists only the publications of national governments, those for Great Britain falling on pages 273–325. A few titles will suggest the range of material included:

Board of Education. General reports of H. M. Inspectors on elementary schools . . . 1886–

Ecclesiastical commissioners for England report 1846–

Pauperism (England and Wales). Monthly comparative returns of paupers relieved . . . 1857–

Entries are arranged alphabetically under the department, bureau, or ministry responsible for the serial; three form headings— census; law reports, etc.; and laws, statutes, etc.—collect a variety of related material into one place for each country.

Another of the monumental enumerative bibliographies produced in the 1930s, the *Cambridge Bibliography of English Literature,* included a good section on nineteenth-century periodicals. This work was the foundation on which Henry and Sheila Rosenberg built the larger and much better listing in the third volume of (20) the *New Cambridge Bibliography of English Literature.* Here, lists of the daily and weekly press, Sunday papers, illustrated papers, agricultural papers, humorous papers, juveniles, magazines and reviews, and the products of school and university journalism—to name some of the categories included— fill almost one hundred tightly packed columns. The names of proprietors and editors are frequently given, along with normal bibliographical information. The Rosenbergs have commented on the difficulties of their work in "Nineteenth-Century Newspapers and Magazines in the *New CBEL*" (*VPN*, 1968), saying that wide as the coverage is, many areas still could not be included or were included by only a representative title or two.

They also regret the uncertainty about some editors and proprietors—information that can be extremely difficult to trace.

Since 1920, bibliographers have learned to be much more cautious about claims to completeness in listing nineteenth-century periodicals. No one knows what "completeness" may be, but we now know enough about the tremendous vitality and diversity of Victorian newspapers and magazines to know how far short previous estimates were and to foresee the search that will be necessary if we are to achieve "completeness." The (21) *Waterloo Directory of Victorian Periodicals 1824–1900: Phase 1* (ed. Michael Wolff, John S. North, and Dorothy Deering, 1976) represents an important first step toward "completeness." The *Waterloo Directory* compiles the information included in the *Times Handlist* (18), Mitchell's *Newspaper Press Directory* (14), the *Union List of Serials* (9), the *British Union Catalogue of Periodicals* (10), Wiener's *Finding List* (44), and the British Museum catalogue of newspapers (4). It reports no data not already recorded in these sources and is above all a reference tool of convenience. However, just by collecting the presently available bibliographic data, the *Directory* puts us in a position for the first time to unravel some problems created by similar and ambiguous titles, to identify conflicting and incomplete bibliographic data, and—most important—to survey the entire field of Victorian periodical publication. There is reason to believe a further survey will uncover more than fifty thousand extant titles. This approximation to "completeness" is the goal of Phase II of the *Directory*, described at the end of this chapter.

RETROSPECTIVE LISTS: REGIONAL

The neglect of the provincial press in the *Times Handlist* reflects a continuing difficulty. The provincial press has always commanded less attention than the metropolitan press, and the bibliographies dealing with it tend to be minor or ephemeral publications that are themselves often hard to identify bibliographically and hard to secure. Moreover, while the difference between a bibliography and a union list is clear enough in the abstract, the distinction between the two often collapses in publications dealing with the regional press. Often the lists deal only with material that is available in specified depositories and thus are union lists; they fall short of the true bibliographic ideal of describing the entire output of a region whether or not the publications are still available there.

This essay presents only a few regional lists. For more of these, readers should consult Section A, pages 6–8, of Lionel Madden and Diana Dixon's *The Nineteenth-Century Periodical Press in Britain: A Bibliography of Modern Studies 1901–1971*, published as a supplement to the *Victorian Periodicals Newsletter* (Sept. 1975), and Chapter iii of this *Guide*. Three rather different lists will suggest the range of material that is available. An extensive series, informally titled (22) "Bibliography of Scottish Periodical Literature," that appeared in *Scottish Notes and Queries* throughout the entire span of its publication reflects the antiquarian interest in periodicals. Readers should consult the index to each volume under "Bibliography" to locate the individual contributions, but a list of the cities and towns covered, along with the appropriate series and volume numbers (but not page numbers), will indicate the scope of the series.

> Aberdeen. Ser. 1, vols. 1–10; Ser. 2, vols. 2–7; Ser. 3, vol. 12.
> Aberdeenshire. Ser. 2, vol. 6.
> Arbroath. Ser. 1, vol. 2.
> Dundee. Ser. 1, vols. 3–4, 6, 9; Ser. 2, vols. 6–7.
> Edinburgh. Ser. 1, vols. 5–6, 8–9, 11; Ser. 2, vols. 1–8;
>   Ser. 3, vols. 8–13.
> Gretna Green. Ser. 3, vols. 9, 12.
> Hawick. Ser. 2, vol. 5.
> Montrose. Ser. 1, vols. 3–4; Ser. 2, vol. 8.
> North Eastern District. Ser. 1, vol. 1.
> Perth. Ser. 2, vol. 8.
> Peterhead. Ser. 1, vols. 2–3.
> Stonehaven. Ser. 1, vols. 2–3.
> West of Scotland. Ser. 1, vol. 1.

An analytical scholarly interest informs a second category of regional lists, represented here by (23) Asa Briggs's *Press and Public in Early Nineteenth-Century Birmingham* (1949). This study includes an annotated checklist of forty-five Birmingham periodicals and newspapers published between 1800 and 1835, only eleven of which are reported in the *Times Handlist*. Librarians, too, are much concerned with the bibliographic control of the provincial periodical press, and various units of the Library Association have published one notable series, mostly designed as location guides to existing files, although it has great bibliographic value in a field not well covered. Chapter iii of this *Guide* describes these publications. Typical of the series is (24) *Newspapers First Published before 1900 in Lancashire, Cheshire and the Isle of Man: A Union List of Holdings in Libraries and Newspaper Offices within That Area*, published by the Library Association, Reference, Special and Information Section, North Western Group and edited by R. E. G. Smith (1964). This list contains 396 newspapers, arranged by town of publication, and gives dates of publication and holdings statements for each.

RETROSPECTIVE LISTS: SPECIFIC SUBJECT FIELDS

There is probably no end to the lists of periodicals concerned with specific subjects. They will be found attached to scholarly studies like Asa Briggs's (23) or independently published throughout the specialized literature that all fields of study generate. A good example of the latter type is (25) Raymond Clare Archibald's "Notes on Some Minor English Mathematical Serials" (*Mathematical Gazette*, 1928), which offers good descriptive accounts of some forty journals of the eighteenth and nineteenth centuries, including "several titles not mentioned in any previous list." Such lists can often be found by starting with the standard bibliographic guides to the field in question. Archibald's article, for instance, is listed in Kenneth O. May's *Bibliography and Research Manual of the History of Mathematics* (1973), along with several other articles that may be useful to the student of mathematical periodicals.

What follows is only a representative list of retrospective bibliographies for periodicals in special fields. It is offered to suggest the variety of lists that can be found and with the hope that presenting these will save at least some students the trouble of hunting them out of the literature. Coverage is so widespread and unsystematic as to frustrate any classified listing of this material.

The list is given in chronological order instead, with cross-references among related items.

(26) Bigmore, E. C., and W. W. H. Wyman. *A Bibliography of Printing.* 1954; a photographic reprint of the 1884 edition. Bigmore and Wyman list periodical publications on the printing arts in Volume II. Their work was based on an earlier bibliography, Louis Mohr, *Die periodische Fachpresse der Typographie und der Verwandten Geschäftszweige* (Strassburg, 1879), but is far richer. See also (31) and (35).

(27) Leiper, Robert Thomson. *Periodicals of Medicine and the Allied Sciences in British Libraries.* 1923. Leiper "aims at an approximately complete list of periodicals (including the serials of learned societies) available in Britain" and includes periodicals in areas related to medicine (e.g., bacteriology, chemistry, anthropology). The periodicals are arranged by language groups, including "English speaking countries and their possessions." See also (30), (61), and (62) .

(28) Fletcher, John R. "Early Catholic Periodicals in England." *Dublin Review* (1936). All but a few of the titles listed are nineteenth-century publications. Editors and publishers are identified.

(29) Sper, Felix. *The Periodical Press of London, Theatrical and Literary (excluding the Daily Newspaper) 1800–1830.* 1937. Sper aimed at comprehensive coverage of all periodicals appearing weekly or less frequently; he has brief notes on editors and contributors. See also (37).

(30) LeFanu, W. R. *British Periodicals of Medicine: A Chronological List.* 1938; rpt. from the *Bulletin of the Institute of the History of Medicine* (1937, 1938). LeFanu lists in chronological order the medical periodicals published in Britain and its colonies from the seventeenth century on. See also (27), (61), and (62).

(31) Ulrich, Carolyn Farquhar, and Karl Küp. *Books and Printing: A Selected List of Periodicals 1800–1942.* Woodstock, Vt.: William E. Rudge, 1943. Ulrich and Küp list periodicals published in all European languages;

many entries are annotated. See also (26) and (35).

(32) Buttress, F. A. *Agricultural Periodicals of the British Isles, 1681–1900, and Their Location.* Cambridge: Univ. of Cambridge School of Agriculture, 1950. This is a handlist of about 450 titles, and no claim to completeness is made. The list excludes titles in botany, economics, forestry, gardening, horticulture, and veterinary science. See also (67).

(33) London University. Institute of Advanced Legal Studies. *A Survey of Legal Periodicals Held in British Libraries.* 1949; 2nd ed., 1957. This survey is a union list; it includes 464 law periodicals of many nations and excludes law reports and a number of specialized periodicals on patent law held by the Patent Office, London. See also (66).

(34) Egoff, Sheila A. *Children's Periodicals of the Nineteenth Century: A Survey and Bibliography.* 1951. The bibliography lists about 850 British titles and includes editors, when known.

(35) Saint Bride Foundation Institute. *Catalogue of the Periodicals Relating to Printing & Allied Subjects in the Technical Library of the Saint Bride Institute.* 1951. The catalogue includes 730 titles, many of which are found in no other British library. The Library opened in 1895 and has a manuscript catalogue of the most important periodical articles. See also (26) and (31).

(36) Brophy, Jacqueline. "Bibliography of British Labor and Radical Journals 1880–1914." *Labor History* (1962). Brophy lists about one hundred journals of all political and economic persuasions and gives brief descriptive annotations. She excludes trade-union journals of very narrow scope and some small provincial publications. A new *Warwick Guide to British Labour Periodicals, 1790–1970,* compiled by Royden Harrison, has been announced as forthcoming (January 1978).

(37) Stratman, Carl J. *Britain's Theatrical Periodicals, 1720–1967: A Bibliography.* 2nd ed., 1972. Stratman lists more than 670 periodicals published in England, Scot-

land, and Ireland, including periodicals concerned
with music halls, vaudeville and the variety theater,
opera and operetta. See also (29).

(38) Fraenkel, Josef. *Exhibition of the Jewish Press in Great Britain, 1823–1963.* 1963. Fraenkel lists 483 Jewish-in-
terest periodicals published in Great Britain in English, Hebrew, Yiddish, and other languages. See also
(42).

(39) Holzapfel, Rudi. "A Survey of Irish Literary Periodicals
from 1900 to the Present Day." Litt.M. Thesis, Trin-
ity Coll., Dublin, 1964. Holzapfel's thesis contains a
few titles begun in the nineteenth century and has
informative annotations for each entry.

(40) Pondrom, Cyrena Norman. "English Literary Periodicals:
1885–1918." Diss. Columbia Univ. 1965. Pondrom
concentrates on avant-garde periodicals, but includes
others as well. Annotations identify editors and assess
the significance of each title.

(41) Fellinger, Imogen. *Verzeichnis der Musikzeitschriften des
19. Jahrhunderts.* Regensburg: Gustav Bosse, 1968.
This massive bibliography covers all Western-lan-
guage periodicals and includes more than two hundred titles published in London alone. British titles
may best be located by using the indexes to place of
publication, to editors, and to publishers and printers.

(42) Prager, Leonard. "A Bibliography of Yiddish Periodicals in
Great Britain (1867–1967) ." *Studies in Bibliography
and Booklore* (1969). The prefatory essays sketch the
history of Yiddish-speaking Jews who migrated to England, especially in the late nineteenth century, and
the creation in London of the Yiddish radical press.
The bibliography includes 201 periodicals published
wholly or in part in Yiddish and excludes literary
miscellanea, theater annuals, press service reports, and
irregular bulletins. See also (38).

(43) Roberts, Helene E. *British Art Periodicals of the Eighteenth
and Nineteenth Centuries. Victorian Periodicals
Newsletter* (1970). Roberts lists 317 periodicals published between 1774 and 1899 and gives a chrono-

logical table of the titles published in any given year
and an index to the editors of art periodicals.

(44) Wiener, Joel. *A Descriptive Finding List of Unstamped British Periodicals 1830–1836.* 1970. Wiener aims at comprehensive coverage of unstamped periodicals published in the early 1830s, excluding periodicals
published monthly or less frequently and those that
sold for sixpence or more. He lists 562 titles, indexes
publishers, printers, editors, and illustrators, and includes a valuable "Partial list of works used."

(45) Gray, Donald J. "A List of Comic Periodicals Published in
Great Britain, 1800–1900, with a Prefatory Essay."
Victorian Periodicals Newsletter (1972). Gray lists
about 450 periodicals and gives brief characterizations
of many of them.

(46) Tye, J. R. *Periodicals of the Nineties: A Checklist of Literary Periodicals Published in the British Isles at
Longer than Fortnightly Intervals, 1890–1899.* 1974.
This checklist excludes professional, trade, sectarian,
and cheap publications and focuses on magazines re-
flecting a "serious" interest in literature per se. It lists
138 titles, with information on publishers, printers,
and editors.

(47) Palmegiano, E. M. *Women and British Periodicals 1832–
1867: A Bibliography. Victorian Periodicals Newsletter* (1976). Section I lists seventy newspapers, magazines, and annuals addressed specifically to women;
Section II identifies nonfiction articles on the Woman
Question from a wide range of general- and special-
interest periodicals. Palmegiano includes a list of editors of women's periodicals.

The Bibliographic Control of
Periodical Contents: Indexing

To have the title of a periodical—or even of all the periodicals
published in nineteenth-century Britain—is only the first step in
bringing periodical literature under bibliographic control. The

second step, which is providing access to the authors and subjects of every piece printed in the periodicals, is exponentially more difficult. Yet it must be taken one way or another if the periodicals are to be kept on the shelves and used by readers. Again, most of the attempts to bring the contents of periodicals under bibliographic control date from about the middle of the nineteenth century, and by the end of the century the British librarian Frank Campbell was saying that journal articles should be handled just as books were. Each article

> must be *catalogued*. And in so saying I am not recommending any startling doctrine, but only one the truth of which is already testified to, not only by the existence of the Royal Society's Catalogue of Scientific Papers, but by the fact that a Modern Bibliography is not considered complete except it contain all the articles connected with the subject which have appeared in Periodicals.

Such was the bibliographic standard by 1896, and in fact some notable catalogues of periodical writings had been produced during the nineteenth century. But most of the bibliographic control of journals was achieved through indexing them. These two approaches, and the librarians' eventual surrender of the work into the hands of indexers and other special-interest groups, established the basis for the division that exists today between librarians and information scientists. But the involvement of librarians in the bibliographic control of periodicals during the second half of the nineteenth century was of decisive importance. Their work and that of a number of special-subject indexers provide virtually the only access to individual essays in Victorian periodicals.

The indexes are of three types: cumulative indexes to individual periodicals, indexes to general-interest periodicals, and indexes and catalogues to the journal literature of special subject fields. No effort is made here to identify many of the first type, cumulative indexes to individual periodicals. (48) *Palmer's Index to the Times Newspaper* (1868–1943; rpt. 1965) is one of a few newspaper indexes and is distinguished by the importance of the newspaper and the period covered (from 1790 to the

present). For indexes to individual magazines, the best list is
(49) Daniel C. Haskell's *A Check List of Cumulative Indexes to
Individual Periodicals in the New York Public Library* (1942).
Haskell attempts to identify all the cumulative indexes available
in the New York Public Library, in all languages and from all
periods; he also sometimes includes indexes not available in the
Library.

To Sampson Low, again, goes the honor of the first attempt at a
current index to more than one general-interest periodical: (50)
the *Index to Current Literature: Comprising a Reference to
Author and Subject of Every Book in the English Language, and
to Original Articles in Literature, Science, and Art, in Serial
Publications* (1860–62). Low's index survived only two years,
but it deserves special attention as a pioneer effort by the book
trade to bring its own productions under bibliographic control.
Low abandoned traditional classified schemes of knowledge and
adopted title-derived subject terms for indexing. It was a good
index, but unfortunately it had to be discontinued in February
1862 for lack of subscriptions—a problem that would plague
indexing efforts for general literature for the next forty years. It
was a disappointed Low who wrote (on the verso of the volume
title page) that the index "was commenced with little expecta-
tion, indeed, of pecuniary reward, but with the impression that
the general utility would be readily acknowledged."

That acknowledgment came later, most notably in America,
amid the burgeoning public library movement. The key figure
here was William Frederick Poole, compiler of the great and now
probably greatly underutilized (51) *Index to Periodical Literature*, always known as *Poole's Index*. Poole produced his first
periodical index in 1848 to meet the needs of his fellow students
at Yale. That index was privately circulated, and a second one
published in 1853 won some recognition but failed to meet its
printing costs. Both these indexes were discrete works, not designed (like Low's) as a continuing index. Poole's work on the
Boston Mercantile Library catalogue and his experience in public
libraries in Cincinnati and Chicago persuaded him of the value of
simple and prompt bibliographic control. The decisive event in
establishing such control over general-interest periodicals was the
adoption of Poole's indexing scheme by the fledgling American

Library Association in 1876; this great cooperative work took fruit in the *Index*, published in 1882.

Poole's Index brings under bibliographic control the contents of 479 British and American periodicals published between 1802 and 1906—a total of about 590,000 articles. For a list of the 190 British periodicals that are indexed, the reader should consult Wayne Somers' "Aids to the Use of *Poole's Index*" (*VPN*, 1970). The *Index* is a monumental achievement, and it is monumentally useful *if* one understands its limitations and is inventive in using it in the way it was designed to be used. The limitations are several. First, and most important, the *Index* is a subject index only and there are, as a result, no author entries. Authors are identified, when known, but there is no direct access to them in the *Index* itself. This deficiency was remedied with the publication of C. Edward Wall's *Cumulative Author Index for Poole's Index to Periodical Literature 1802–1906* (1971). This is a computer-produced index to the 300,000 author references in Poole, but Wall made no effort to verify or to regularize the forms of the names. Users must therefore search names under all their possible spellings, under variant entry elements (this is especially important with hyphenated names and names beginning with prepositions), under variant transliterations, and under variant titles of nobility. Wall cautions that "less obvious possibilities [for variation] are numerous . . . and should be checked to the limits of one's imagination." A second difficulty in using *Poole's Index* is that all articles not having a distinct subject matter (e.g., works of fiction, poems, plays) are entered under the first word in their titles that is not an article. Book reviews are indexed under the subject of the book reviewed; when the book has no subject (e.g., works of imaginative literature) the book reviewed is entered under its author.

The third, and greatest, difficulty in using *Poole's Index* derives from the fact that the subject terms under which articles are indexed were derived from the titles of the articles themselves, and little effort was made to direct readers from one term to others that are related. Wall's caution about searching for authors applies with double force in subject searches: possible points of entry are numerous, and they should be checked to the limits of the user's imagination. As an illustration, this author conducted a sample search of the articles published in 1871 about the Paris Commune that are listed in the *Wellesley Index* to discover under what subject entries these articles are found. Twenty-seven articles listed in the *Wellesley Index* for 1871 are unambiguously concerned with the Commune. There may be others, with titles that do not indicate their content (a problem in any title-based search, whether in *Poole's Index* or the *Wellesley Index*), and it is always difficult to decide where one subject gives way to another—where the Commune gives way to the Siege of Paris, or where either gives way to the Franco-Prussian War. So for the purposes of this demonstration, the twenty-seven unambiguous cases were taken as the "complete" list. All but one of them could be found under the following headings in *Poole's Index*:

Commune	and the English working class	1
	and the International	1
	in Paris (with several further subheadings)	13*
France	finance in in 1871	1
	history of Franco-Prussian War week in Paris	1*
	history of 1870–81	1*
	politics of in 1871	3
International Working-Men's Association		1
Paris	in 1588–94 Commune vs. King	1
	in 1871	1
	seige of	2
	week in	1*
	workmen of, and the commune	1

* Includes one entry that refers to two different essays, and two essays entered under two headings each in *Poole's Index*.

Most of these entries are obvious enough, and one need only glance over the subdivisions in *Poole's Index*—especially those under France and Paris—to get quickly to the most likely entry points. Two essays are listed under more than one entry each, but the essay commenting on the Commune by comparing it with a sixteenth-century uprising ("Paris in 1588–94") would most likely not be found except in the most exhaustive search of *Poole's Index*. One essay listed in the *Wellesley Index*, titled "Paris and France," does not appear under any of the above terms or under a number of others that were searched. The *Index* sends the reader on one fruitless search because of an erroneous entry: an article listed under "France in 1871, Condition of" turns out to have been published in 1869.

Nearly half of the relevant essays, thus, are listed in one place in *Poole's Index*, with the others scattered under more or less obvious entry points. The entries used by Poole—usually adopted from titles, but sometimes constructed to reflect content—lead to no irrelevant articles. There is some inconsistency in choice of entry term, and few cross-references or double entries. Still, on a relatively discrete subject like the Paris Commune, *Poole's Index* works quite well—if one perseveres. Subjects of broader scope would most likely involve a wider variety of terms and require a more agile imagination.

A further difficulty in using the *Index* is the simple frustration of finding only the first page of an article identified, not the inclusive page numbers, and of finding that the volume numbers Poole gives often have no bearing on the volume numbers one can expect to find on library shelves. Poole objected to publishers' vagaries in serial numbering and created a simple, consecutive numbering scheme for each title he indexed—thereby creating problems for every user of the *Index*. Readers can turn to one of three aids for making the necessary translation of numbers: the "Chronological Conspectus of the Serials Indexed" provided in the *Index* itself (though to use this, one must first secure yet another number for the desired title from an alphabetical listing of "Abbreviations, Titles, and Imprints"); or, more simply, either Marion V. Bell and Jean C. Bacon's *Poole's Index Date and Volume Key* (1957) or Vinton A. Dearing's *Transfer Vectors for Poole's Index to Periodical Literature* (1967). Both of these works are easily used, but to have to use them at all is a nuisance.

Poole planned to issue annual supplements to the *Index* but was able, as it turned out, to publish supplements at only five-year intervals. To provide current indexing, Poole's associate, W. I. Fletcher, began issuing (52) the *Co-operative Index to Periodicals*, at first as a monthly supplement to the *Library Journal* (Mar. 1883–Jan. 1885), then separately each quarter (1885–89), though with a considerable increase in the number of periodicals indexed, and then finally as an annual (1890–1911).

Fletcher's index was successively retitled the *Annual Literary Index* (1892–1904) and the *Annual Library Index* (1905–10). Fletcher indexed authors as well as subjects from 1887 on. His indexes were no less useful than Poole's, but no more successful financially. This plea and admonition from Melvil Dewey suggests how precarious Fletcher's venture was when it first appeared as a separate publication:

> I appeal to the intelligent and reasonable librarians who really wish to see our profession elevated to a higher rank, our methods improved, our expenses reduced by co-operation, while our usefulness steadily increases, to stand by the men who have done for us in the past, and will continue to do, unless we blindly force them out of our service by a penny-wise policy that enables us to sponge the benefits this year, but cuts us off from getting them at any price hereafter.
>
> We have not yet attained to the doctrine that the laborer is worthy of his hire, but are striving for that lower plane, where we preach that the laborer who works for nothing is worthy of having his actual expenses paid by those who reap the benefits of his services.

Fletcher's annual index did not meet the need for current information, so the Cleveland Public Library began to publish the index it had for some time been preparing for its own patrons. The (53) *Cumulative Index to a Selected List of Periodicals* first appeared in 1896, but, again, high publication costs and too few subscribers forced this monthly index to quarterly publication in 1899; in 1903 it was abandoned altogether. All of the titles in Fletcher's indexes and in the *Cumulative Index* were also indexed—if less promptly—in Poole.

The situation was no more promising in Great Britain. The only British index to general periodicals was (54) W. T. Stead's *Annual Index of Periodicals and Photographs* (1898–1902), also known as the *Review of Reviews Index*. Stead was trying to do for British readers what Poole had done for Americans, except that his was a commercial publishing venture from the start and did not involve British librarians cooperatively. Stead's *Index* includes a large number of British periodicals of the 1890s that are not indexed in *Poole's Index*. In its first number it also indexed photographs and other visual arts publications and published a useful list and description of the principal periodicals. The only other British guide to general magazines of this period is (55) Alfred Cotgreave's *Contents-Subject Index to General and Periodical Literature* (1900), a one-time index that is highly selective and remarkable mostly for its inclusion of essays published in books as well as in periodicals.

Two other indexes should be mentioned. (56) The *Magazine Subject-Index* (comp. Frederick Winthrop Faxon, 1909–21) indexes one English journal, the *Windsor Magazine* (London, 1895–), that is not included in *Poole's Index*. The second index is an entire library-service enterprise carried on by William Mc-Crillis Griswold. Griswold produced a plethora of indexes and reader advisory publications between 1880 and 1898. His (57) *Q. P. Indexes* (Bangor, Me.: Q. P. Index, 1880–86) began publication with "An Analytical Index to the Political Contents of 'The Nation' . . . 1865–1880" and included cumulative indexes to several other periodicals, as well as an annual "Cumulative Index" of several journals (1881–85).

All the above indexes were produced contemporaneously, or nearly so, with the journals they indexed. They reflect the oddities always present in pioneering ventures and the compromises that must be made to provide current information while it is still current. Uneven and eccentric as some of them are, they are virtually our only means of subject access to nineteenth-century journals that addressed a general audience. Retrospective indexing is a rare undertaking. Two specially valuable retrospective indexes merit attention here. The first is (58) the *Nineteenth Century Readers' Guide to Periodical Literature, 1890–1899* (ed. Helen Grant Cushing and Adah V. Morris, 1944). This index covers only fifty-one periodicals, but seven of them are not in *Poole's Index*; two of these seven are British titles, the London *Bookman* and the *Yellow Book*. The *Nineteenth Century Readers' Guide* differs from *Poole's Index* in using standardized, verified author entries and in using a standard list of subject headings, instead of title-derived indexing entries. Work on the index was discontinued when it was published, leaving us only the hope expressed by Cushing (p. vii) that the index could be pushed further back into the century. A second venture is (59) the *Wellesley Index to Victorian Periodicals* (1966–). This is primarily an index to authors, most of them anonymous until the Houghtons and their associates penetrated the recesses of nineteenth-century publishing history. Chapter vii of this *Guide* describes the *Wellesley Index* fully, but it is pertinent here too because Part A of the *Index* gives direct chronological access to the contents of the most prestigious Victorian periodicals and could be made the basis for subject access as well.

So far this essay has described only the indexes to general-interest periodicals that came into being primarily as a part of an increasingly professional public library service in America. There are, in addition, quite a number of indexes to the periodical literature of special-interest groups—produced, usually, as an activity of the professional organizations of the groups involved. These indexes, like the special-subject periodical lists described in the first part of this paper, are best found by exploring the literature of individual fields. Readers should be particularly alert to a wide range of nineteenth-century indexes produced in Germany that encompassed journals written in English and other foreign languages. The following list includes, with one exception, only the indexes produced in Britain or America that offered extensive coverage of English-language material.

(60) The Royal Society of London. *Catalogue of Scientific Papers, 1800–1900.* 1867–1902. This is a monumental index, in seventeen volumes, of 1,555 periodicals in many languages. The entries are arranged by author; subject access is provided by a separate, three-volume *Catalogue of Scientific Papers, 1800–1900 Subject Index* (1908–14). This subject index is incomplete, providing access to only about 116,000 articles in mathematics, "Mechanics," and physics.

(61) *Index Medicus.* 1879–1922. *Index Medicus* appeared monthly from January 1879; it suspended publication from April 1899 through December 1902, during which period the Institut de Bibliographie in Paris published a similar index, *Bibliotheca medica.* See also (27), (30), and (62).

(62) United States. Surgeon General's Office. Library. *Index-Catalogue of the Library of the Surgeon-General's Office, United States Army.* 1880–95. A second series covers the period 1896–1915. This is an author-subject catalogue of books, pamphlets, and periodical articles. A separate publication of the same office, an *Alphabetical List of Abbreviations of Titles of Medical Periodicals Employed in the Index-Catalogue* (1895) is a useful inventory of medical titles. See also (27), (30), and (61).

(63) *Repertorium der technischen Journal-Literatur, 1879–99.* Berlin: Heymann, 1881–1900. Most of the journals indexed are German, though there are several English and French journals as well. This index was published as *Repertorium der technischen Literatur* from 1823 to 1879. See (64) and (65).

(64) Galloupe, Francis Ellis. *An Index to Engineering Periodicals, 1883–1892, Comprising Engineering; Railroads; Science; Manufactures and Trade.* 1888–93. Volume I indexes nineteen American and British periodicals by subject; Volume II indexes twenty-four periodicals and a number of general periodicals that are covered for their engineering articles. See (63) and (65).

(65) *Engineering Index, 1884–1905.* 1892–1906. Volume I (1884–91) reprints the monthly index published in the *Journal of the Association of Engineering Societies*. Volume II (1892–95) indexes sixty-two journals, most of them in English; Volume III (1896–1900) indexes nearly two hundred journals in several languages. See (63) and (64).

(66) Jones, Leonard Augustus. *Index to Legal Periodical Literature.* 1888–99. Volume I indexes 158 law journals and reviews, and aims at covering all legal periodicals in English published before January 1887. Legal articles in 113 nonlegal periodicals are indexed, and special attention is given to biographical articles on judges and lawyers. Volume II (1887–90) broadens the scope of coverage to include legislation, political science, economics, and sociology. Volume III covers the

years 1898 to 1907, but indexes only sixty periodicals. See also (33).

(67) United States. Dept. of Agriculture. U.S. Experiment Stations. *Experiment Station Record, 1889–1922.* 1890–1922. The *Record* is an abstract journal, concerned primarily with the reports of U.S. experimental stations. It also includes numerous digests and abstracts of British periodical publications under the heading "Foreign Investigations." Author and subject indexes provide access to this material. See also (32).

(68) Gomme, Sir George Laurence. *Index of Archaeological Papers 1665–1890.* 1907. Continued by the *Index of Archaeological Papers Published in 1891–1910.* 1892–1914. The primary interest served is that of British local history and British antiquities. Gomme indexes ninety-four periodicals, which included some classical and non-British subjects as well.

(69) Richardson, Ernest Cushing. *An Alphabetical Subject Index and Index Encyclopedia to Periodical Articles on Religion, 1890–1899.* 1907–11. Richardson models his index after Poole; most of the periodicals covered are not British.

(70) Boyle, Andrew. *An Index to the Annuals.* Worcester, Eng.: A. Boyle, 1967. Boyle indexes about twenty-five annuals published between 1820 and 1850 to identify anonymous and pseudonymous contributions. A second, posthumous volume will be published by Chadwyck-Healey, Ltd., Cambridge.

(71) *Index of Economic Articles in Journals and Collective Volumes.* Homewood, Ill.: R. D. Irwin, 1961–. The first volume of this continuing index covers English-language journals published between 1886 and 1924, including many general-interest periodicals. But only three British titles that began publication before 1900 are indexed.

(72) Sader, Marion. *Comprehensive Index to English-Language Little Magazines 1890–1970. Series One.* 8 vols. 1976. This index covers one hundred titles, about twenty-five of which are British publications. Sader indexes

works by and about individuals; there is no subject indexing.

An Academy of Projectors

It is an article of faith among librarians that, with respect to bibliographic control, more is truly better. From this faith springs the dream of universal bibliographic control. Those who pursue such dreams—even for so relatively limited a field as Victorian periodicals—are liable to the often encountered view of bibliographers: that they are harmless drudges, of some use, but members—albeit pleasant ones—of the Lagado Academy of Projectors. The elusive Cornelius Walford, whose house and the adjoining one were packed full of the periodicals that he hoped someday to bring under bibliographic control, is the paradigm of the bibliographic projector in serials. Some visionary projects, however, are carried through to completion, against all odds. These last pages are devoted to past and present perspectives on the bibliographic control of nineteenth-century periodicals; they record some previous bibliographic surveys and a few works of high, if tangential, interest to the subject, and then make a very few projections about the future of the bibliography of Victorian periodicals.

No other essay details as many of the bibliographic works pertinent to nineteenth-century periodicals as this one. Students will, however, want to consult a few essays of similar scope for their different insights. Walter Houghton describes the major bibliographic tools, the difficulties of using *Poole's Index*, and the earliest plans for his own *Wellesley Index* in a fine essay, (73) "British Periodicals of the Victorian Age: Bibliographies and Indexes" (*Library Trends*, 1959). The third chapter of (74) Lionel Madden's excellent bibliographic guide, *How to Find Out about the Victorian Period* (1970), gives good directions for the use of the major sources. And Paul E. Vesenyi provides an overview of the bibliographic control of periodicals in his (75) *An Introduction to Periodical Bibliography* (1974). Readers of this book will be particularly interested in Vesenyi's fourth chapter, which is devoted to the nineteenth century and has a good account of European (especially German) periodical indexing. Vesenyi also has a bibliography of periodical bibliographies that he consciously weights in favor of the humanities and social sciences, though most of the items are current and thus not concerned with nineteenth-century periodicals.

There are a number of other reference works that are tangential to Victorian periodicals and that researchers are likely to know in other connections. The potential importance of these may be suggested by a most unsystematically chosen sample of them:

(76) *Bulletin of Bibliography.* 1897–   . The Boston Book Company specialized in supplying both current and retrospective periodicals to libraries. Frederick W. Faxon edited the company's *Bulletin,* which offers a wealth of miscellaneous but valuable bibliographic lore—including Faxon's series on "Magazine Perplexities," the identification of some anonymous writers of articles indexed by Poole, a "births and deaths" record of new, changed, and expired periodical titles, a bibliography of literary annuals and gift books, and many other features. The *Bulletin* is indexed in *Bulletin of Bibliography and Magazine Notes Cumulative Index,* compiled by Eleanor Cavanaugh Jones and Margaret L. Pollard (1977).

(77) Goss, Charles W. F. *The London Directories, 1677–1855: A Bibliography with Notes on Their Origin and Development.* 1932. A great number of people associated with the production of periodicals are difficult to trace. The directories to London and other Victorian cities are gratifyingly useful in locating people and ascertaining business connections.

(78) Weed, Katherine Kirtley, and Richmond Pugh Bond, "Studies of British Newspapers and Periodicals from Their Beginning to 1800: A Bibliography." *Studies in Bibliography* (1946). This is the standard bibliography of secondary works for the pre-Victorian era and a most impressive work. The Madden-Dixon bibliography of secondary works for the Victorian era has already been

mentioned. The *New Cambridge Bibliography of English Literature*, Volume III, identifies much secondary material contemporary with the periodicals themselves, as do Richard Altick's wonderfully rich pioneer study *The English Common Reader* (1957) and Robert B. White's *The English Literary Journal to 1900: A Guide to Information Sources* (1977). William S. Ward's *British Periodicals & Newspapers, 1789–1832: A Bibliography of Secondary Sources* (1973) is especially good for the period it covers.

(79) Price, Warren C. *The Literature of Journalism: An Annotated Bibliography.* 1959. Another standard work, Price's bibliography is limited to English-language material and is concerned primarily with American journalism. There are nevertheless many entries for a wide range of British subjects, and some two hundred entries in the section on "Bibliographies and Directories." No one seeking information on Victorian periodicals should fail to consult Price.

(80) Marconi, Joseph V. *Indexed Periodicals: A Guide to 170 Years of Coverage in 33 Indexing Services.* 1976. This is a convenient guide to indexed periodicals, though only four of the indexes Marconi lists cover nineteenth-century journals.

The several dozen works described in this chapter have established both what the bibliographic control of Victorian periodicals is and what it will become. These works are the basis from which further bibliographic control will develop. Two challenging projects presently under way must be mentioned here, along with this writer's idea of our next horizon in periodicals bibliography.

The Houghtons' *Wellesley Index to Victorian Periodicals* has been the inspiration of a new generation of students. In this chapter little is said of the *Wellesley Index*, as its main contribution has been authorship attribution, the concern of Chapter vii of this *Guide*. Nonetheless, when the Houghtons first projected their *Index* they recognized the need for greatly improved subject indexing of periodical literature. And, as they have pointed out, some of the material for this project is readily available in the contents displays that make up Part A of each volume of their *Index*. These displays stand as a challenge to develop a workable scheme for retrospective subject analysis. Projectors of such work may be able to take as a model the *Combined Retrospective Index Sets*—or the inevitable acronym, CRIS (1977). This innovative retrospective index covers about five hundred journal titles in history, political science, and sociology, and is based on the NEXUS data base. Still another computer-assisted index is under way for nineteenth-century American art periodicals. It is clear, then, that methods for computer-assisted retrospective indexing are available. It lies with us to do what Poole and his associates did a century ago, to create a cooperative network for doing the work and, equally important, a market to support the publication and use of such indexes.

If the difficulties of indexing reduce us to acronyms and a dependence on computers, the difficulties of listing all the periodicals the Victorians published elevate us to metaphors of pearls, golden streams, walruses, carpenters, and the infinitude of sand. From this has grown the *Waterloo Directory of Victorian Periodicals* (21), a second monumental work published in recent years on the bibliographic control of periodicals. The first phase of the *Directory* is simply (more or less) a conflation of bibliographic information from several previous works in the field. This compilation enables us for the first time to see something of the true scope and number of Victorian periodicals; to establish an outline or profile of periodical publication in the nineteenth century; to understand how much we do not know, bibliographically, and how much of what we thought we knew is incomplete or self-contradictory; and to comprehend how Herculean a task it will be to untangle and complete our bibliographic knowledge of Victorian periodicals. There is no escaping computers here, either, but most of the work will be a laborious, manual, shelf check of periodicals. A series of articles and reports by Dorothy Deering, John S. North, and Michael Wolff published in the *Victorian Periodicals Newsletter* gives the history and prospects of the *Waterloo Directory*; searching reviews have appeared by Sheila Rosenberg (*VPN*, 1977) and Hans de Groot (*VS*, 1978). The success of the projected second phase of the *Waterloo Direc-*

tory will depend on our ability to document the value of the information we have and to develop a model for the on-site analysis of periodical runs. We must also develop an effective network of cooperating scholars for reporting the data. Such networks are never easy to build or to keep functioning. Phase I of the *Directory* has taken the work as far, probably, as individual effort can. The Research Society for Victorian Periodicals has established an advisory committee for Phase II, with members in both North America and Great Britain charged with developing plans for the future. It is a project that stirs the bibliographer's heart, and one that would have comforted Cornelius Walford, though we can draw little comfort from his experience with the same project.

These projects reflect the two primary functions in the bibliographic control of periodicals—those of indexing and of inventorying. One can always hope for more of both, and more would be genuinely useful. But is there anything else that needs to be projected? This writer believes the next bibliographic horizon for periodicals will involve analytical bibliography and textual analysis. The prevailing assumption seems to be that any given copy of a periodical will be bibliographically identical with any other one of the same date. Such an assumption would discredit any book-centered study, but it seems to go unexamined—or worse, unrealized—in periodical studies. Yet most students of periodicals know even now it is an unsupportable assumption. This writer first discovered it so as a graduate student, when he could not find a copy of J. G. Lockhart's infamous "Chaldee MS" in *Blackwood's Magazine*, where the bibliographies said it was, because, at first unknowingly, he was looking at a state of the magazine in which the piece had been suppressed and replaced by an innocuous article of no interest (then). Other "periodical perplexities" could be cited: ones arising from the absence, during most of the century, of an international copyright law between America and Great Britain, from a diplomatically sensitive phrase about Germany in the *Saturday Review*, from the difficulty the Wilde scandal posed for the editors of the *Yellow Book*. The analytical bibliography of periodicals will hold much of interest for students of individual texts. But because the bibliographer—especially the historical bibliographer—is concerned with the transmission of information as well, the range of interest is in fact much broader.

The timorous bibliographer may feel somewhat ill at ease in the post-Gutenberg era—if that is what we have. Still, we need not go back very far to revel in a time when all mass communication was effected through the printed, and very largely through the periodically printed, word. Anyone who understands the tie between formal bibliographic analysis and the study of how a society communicates with itself will find projects enough to put the Grand Academy at Lagado truly to shame.

In completing (if one dare use that word) the inventory and indexing work that was begun a hundred years ago and in extending our bibliographic inquiry into the physical means of all mass communication in the nineteenth century, we declare ourselves to be heirs of Poole, of the projectors at the Royal Society, of Charles Mitchell and Cornelius Walford, and of all the others for whom Bowker so proudly spoke when he claimed that the organization of knowledge would be a chief glory of the nineteenth century and one of its principal gifts to the twentieth century.

III

Finding Lists for Victorian Periodicals

J. Don Vann and Rosemary T. VanArsdel

North Texas State University
University of Puget Sound

Scholars who find it necessary to make use of Victorian periodical literature in their research are often faced with difficulty in locating copies of the desired sources. Certain basic references for solving this problem are available in British, Canadian, and American libraries.

Major References

The *British Union Catalogue of Periodicals* ([*BUCOP*], 4 vols., with 2 supplements, 1955) is subtitled *A Record of the Periodicals of the World, from the Seventeenth Century to the Present Day, in British Libraries*. This catalogue, covering the holdings of 441 British libraries, generally excludes newspapers first published after 1799 and variant issues of periodicals. It does include yearbooks and other annual publications. Holdings are coded with a precise, yet detailed, system (p. xx) explaining whether a particular library's holdings are complete or broken, and imperfect volumes are identified. The library symbols (pp. xxi–xxxi) show the lending policies of individual institutions so that the prospective borrower knows whether a periodical is available on loan through the interlibrary lending system, whether it may be used only in the borrower's library, or whether it may be checked out for home use. The symbols also show whether the materials are available for reference to the public, to "individuals suitably introduced," or to members only, and whether such materials may be copied by microfilm or by other copying methods. The two supplements to the *BUCOP* (1956–60 and 1960–62) consist principally of new titles appearing in the periods covered by each, but they also include some amended entries to the main volumes, especially new holdings. The *BUCOP Journal*, a quarterly with annual cumulations, supplies further supplements, beginning with 1964.

The *Union List of Serials in Libraries of the United States and Canada* (3rd ed., 5 vols., 1965), has grown from the first edition of 1927, which covered the holdings of 225 libraries, through two supplements (1931 and 1932), a second edition in 1943, to the present edition, reporting the holdings of 956 libraries. The list of cooperating libraries (pp. i-iv) codes each institution's policies on open or restricted lending of the actual serials and on photo-copying or microfilming. The following classes of serials are generally excluded: administrative reports of societies, universities, corporations, etc.; almanacs and gift books; American news-papers; law reports and digests; publications of local, religious, labor, and fraternal organizations; boards of trade publications; news organs of national and international conferences and congresses; house organs, unless of technical or scientific value; and alumni, graduate, and intercollegiate fraternity publications. Although the exclusion of English newspapers published after 1820 is noted in a prefatory statement, a surprising number are included.

Both the *Union List of Serials* and *BUCOP* restrict their listings to larger libraries to avoid becoming too bulky to be workable. The researcher should, therefore, also consult regional library lists, which will be discussed later in this chapter.

The scholar working in the British Library will find the periodical holdings of the Library listed in Volumes 184–86 of the *British Museum General Catalogue of Printed Books*. The printed catalogue is inevitably out-of-date, so the investigator who is on the spot will, of course, consult the paste-up circular catalogue in the Reading Room. Periodicals are entered by the place of publication and are cross-indexed by title. Although a few newspapers are listed, they are for the most part excluded, so that one must consult the *Catalogue of the Newspaper Library, Colindale,* published by the British Library Board (8 vols., 1975). It contains entries for the half-million volumes of daily and weekly newspapers in the Newspaper Library at Colindale. Because the researcher may be seeking either a specific title or the newspapers of a particular locality, the catalogue contains two sets of entries as follows:

Volume I. London
  (a) National newspapers published in London since 1801
  (b) Local newspapers of the thirty-three boroughs of the Greater London area
Volume II. England and Wales, Scotland, Ireland
  (a) Local newspapers entered under the places in which they circulate or in which they were published
  (b) Publications of the armed forces of the United Kingdom, regardless of place of publication
  (c) Ships' newspapers
Volumes III and IV. Overseas countries
Volumes V–VIII. Alphabetical title catalogue
  An alphabetical arrangement of all the titles in Volumes I–IV

This catalogue has been desperately needed by those unable to go to the British Library to use the paste-up catalogue there, for the only published source was the supplement to the older *British Museum Catalogue of Printed Books,* a volume entitled *Newspapers Published in Great Britain and Ireland 1801–1900* (1905). This supplement is so inadequate and full of inaccuracies that it was of little use to scholars.

Another source, the *Times Tercentenary Handlist of English and Welsh Newspapers, Magazines, and Reviews,* represented a complete catalogue of the British Museum's holdings in 1920, but again, one should consult the current catalogue in the Reading Room.

For a limited time span, one might consult William S. Ward, *Index and Finding List of Serials Published in the British Isles*

1789–1832 (1953). Although this work covers only a part of the period presented in this guide, it is nevertheless a valuable source.

Other Finding Lists for Great Britain

The number of regional and specialized finding lists for files of periodicals in England is almost overwhelming. Often merely typewritten and mimeographed, these lists are sometimes difficult to obtain because of their limited circulation. For example, William Myson, in the preface to his *Surrey Newspapers*, noted that only eighty copies of his handlist were to be printed. A microfilm publisher could perform a great service for students of Victorian periodicals by bringing all of these lists together in a cheap microfilm edition.

LONDON

In addition to the *British Museum Catalogue* and the newspaper supplement, the researcher will find useful guides in the *London Union List of Periodicals* (1969), which locates periodical files in thirty-two London boroughs and the libraries of Brighton, Luton, Reading, and Southend-on-Sea, and in the *Westminster City Libraries Union List of Periodicals* (1970), which lists the holdings of fourteen libraries.

Finally, one may consult J. R. Tye, *Periodicals of the Nineties: A Checklist of Literary Periodicals Published at Longer than Fortnightly Intervals 1890–1899* (1974). This is a listing of 137 periodicals, with locations of runs and a useful list of publishers, printers, and editors.

REGIONAL LISTS (BRITISH)

In the past, many individual libraries and groups of small libraries compiled handlists of their periodical holdings. More recently the Library Association has done a splendid job of sponsoring such compilations. Those listed below are often useful for locating regional newspapers that failed to find their way into the British Library Newspaper Library.

Co-operative Filing of Periodicals in Bridgwater, Taunton, Weston-super-Mare and Yeovil Public Libraries. 1953. A listing of two hundred periodicals.

Periodical Publications Currently Displayed in the Coventry Public Libraries. Comp. Lydia A. Beasley. 1925. 623 periodicals in ten locations.

Barnes, Fred, and James L. Hobbs. *Handlist of Newspapers Published in Cumberland, Westmoreland, and North Lancashire.* 1951.

Thwaite, Mary F. *Herefordshire Newspapers, 1772–1955.* 1956. Alphabetical and chronological listing of ninety-nine newspapers.

Kent Union List of Periodicals. Ed. B. Bishop and C. Earl. Library Association, 1969.

Dixon, Diana. *Local Newspapers and Periodicals of the Nineteenth Century: A Checklist of Holdings in Provincial Libraries.* 2 vols. 1973.

Madden, Lionel. *Periodicals in Leicester.* 2 vols. 1969.

Newspapers First Published before 1900 in Lancashire, Cheshire, and the Isle of Man. Library Association, 1964. 396 titles in 103 locations.

Union List of Periodical Files in the Public and Special Libraries of North-East Lancashire. 1959.

A Short Title List of Periodical Holdings in the [Manchester] Reference Libraries. 1955.

Credland, W. R. *The Manchester Free Public Libraries.* 1899. Newspaper and periodical files are listed on pp. 242–46.

Donkin, W. C., and E. Patterson. "Union List of Periodicals," *Literary and Philosophical Society of Newcastle upon Tyne Quarterly Record* (1928). Locates files for 1,800 periodicals.

Union List of Newspaper Files in the Northern Area. Library Association, 1958.

Sheffield Interchange Organization [SINTO] Union List of Periodicals. 1970. Includes the holdings of sixty-six libraries in the Sheffield area.

Brooke, L. E. J. *Somerset Newspapers: 1725–1960.* 1960. Alphabetical as well as chronological arrangement of 181 titles, of which 159 fall into the 1824–1900 period.

Myson, William. *Surrey Newspapers.* 1961. 215 newspapers in twenty-nine libraries.

Scottish Newspapers

Bulloch, John Malcolm. "Files of the Local Press, Past and Present." *Scottish Notes and Queries* (1896).

Ferguson, Joan P. S. *Scottish Newspapers Held in Scottish Libraries.* 1956. 380 newspapers in forty-six libraries.

Irish Periodicals

Ó Casaide, Séamus. *A Guide to Old Waterford Newspapers.* 1917. Holdings in twenty collections.

List of Scientific and Technical Periodicals in Dublin Libraries. 1929.

List of Medical Periodicals Preserved in the Libraries of Ireland. King and Queen's College of Physicians, 1911.

Commonwealth

Commonwealth newspapers are compiled by Arthur R. Hewitt in *Union List of Commonwealth Newspapers in London, Oxford, and Cambridge* (1960), a geographical arrangement of 2,426 titles in sixty-two libraries.

University Libraries

University libraries have been depositories for a considerable number of periodicals. In 1937 the Joint Standing Committee on Library Co-Operation attempted a comprehensive list in the *Union Catalogue of Periodical Publications in the University Libraries of the British Isles,* with entries for 23,115 periodicals in 113 libraries. Lists have also been prepared for the holdings of individual university libraries, the largest number of lists being concentrated in the libraries of the University of London:

University of London Library List of Periodicals. 1956.

Institute of Advanced Legal Studies. *Union List of Periodicals.* 1968.

College of St. Mark and St. John Library. *A Union List of the Periodicals of the Area Colleges of the London Institute of Education.* 1959.

Imperial College of Science and Technology. *Periodical and Serial Holdings.* 1961.

British Postgraduate Medical Federation. *Union List of Periodicals in the Libraries of the Postgraduate Medical School.* . . . 1955.

Lists for other university libraries are:

Oxford University. *Catalogue of Transactions of Societies, Periodicals, and Memoirs Available for the Use of Students in the Reading Room of the Radcliffe Library.* 1887. Transactions of societies, some of which are serial, are on pp. 1–14; periodicals of Great Britain and Ireland are on pp. 42–53.

Catalogue of the Periodical Publications in the Libraries of the University of Bristol. Comp. J. Shum Cox. 1940.

A Union List of Periodicals in the Learned Libraries of Durham. Comp. G. S. Darlow. 1962.

Liverpool University. *A Hand-List of Academies and Periodical Publications in the University Libraries.* . . . 1913. Holdings in twenty-one collections.

Middlesex Technical Colleges. *Union List of Periodicals and Annual Publications.* 1960.

Welsh National School of Medicine. *List of Periodicals in General and Departmental Libraries.* 1954.

SPECIALIZED

Finally, there are lists of periodicals on specialized topics:

Agriculture

Agricultural Periodicals of the British Isles, 1681–1900, and Their Locations. Ed. F. A. Buttress. 1950. Locates files in fifteen collections.

Botanical Periodicals in London Libraries. 1954. 417 periodicals in seventeen libraries.

Anthropology

Royal Anthropological Institute of Great Britain and Ireland. *Survey of Anthropological Journals and Monograph Series in Libraries in the United Kingdom.* 1957.

Architecture

Guppy, Henry, and Guthrie Vine. *A Classified Catalogue of the Works on Architecture and the Allied Arts in the Principal Libraries of Manchester and Salford.* 1909. Periodicals and some society publications in serial on pp. 40–48.

Classical Studies

Southan, Joyce E. *A Survey of Classical Periodicals.* 1962.

Jewish Studies

Fraenkel, Josef. *Exhibition of the Jewish Press in Great Britain, 1823–1963.* 1963. Locates 483 items in four London libraries, three libraries in the United States, and three in Jerusalem.

Mathematics

London Mathematical Association. *Catalogue of Current Mathematical Journals.* 1913.
Union List of Periodicals on Mathematics and Allied Subjects in London Libraries. 1968. Holdings of thirty-seven libraries.

Medicine

LeFanu, William R. *British Periodicals of Medicine.* 1938. Rpt. from the *Bulletin of the Institute of the History of Medicine.* Section 1 contains titles of periodicals that began publication before 1900.
Leiper, Robert T., H. M. Williams, and G. Z. L. LeBas. *Periodicals of Medicine and the Allied Sciences in British Libraries. . . .* 1923. Shows holdings for thirty-seven libraries.

Science

Royal Society of London. *Catalogue of Scientific Papers, 1800–
    1900.* 17 vols. 1867–1902. *Subject Index.* 3 vols. 1908–14.
    Indexes serial publications and identifies locations.

*Union List of Scientific and Technical Periodicals in Northern
    Libraries.* Comp. T. D. Wilson and A. Wallace. Library Asso-
    ciation, 1963.

Regional Lists in Canada and the United States

Research scholars in Victorian periodicals will find it worth
their while to consult whatever regional lists of library holdings
they can locate. The regional lists form the ideal supplement to
the larger lists, such as the *Union List of Serials* and *BUCOP*,
because they include fewer libraries; they can therefore be more
inclusive both in institutions surveyed and in titles listed, and
these lists, because of their lower costs, can be revised more frequently. One interesting example is the one presently being
compiled by the Victorian Studies Association of Western Canada, through articles published in its *Newsletter*. The first issue
(Fall 1972) contained a bibliography of Victorian periodicals at
the University of Calgary. This was followed by similar articles
for the University of Alberta, the McPherson Library at the
University of Victoria, the University of British Columbia, and
for the combined collections of the University of Washington and
the Seattle Public Library (1973–77). In the words of the editor,
Ian Gordon-Craig, "although the *Newsletter* is certainly not
devoted solely to library lists, it is apparent that our original
survey has now become a continuing project and one which need
not necessarily be restricted to University libraries" (1975).

Additionally, the scholar in Canada should see the *Union List
of Non-Canadian Newspapers Held by Canadian Libraries* (ed.
Stephen Rush, 1968), with its list of newspapers from Great
Britain (pp. 9–17).

Similar regional lists available in the United States include the
*Union List of Serials in the Libraries of the State University of
New York* (1967), *A Union List of Serials in the Libraries of the
Consortium of Libraries of the Metropolitan Washington D.C.*

Area (1967), and the *Union List of Periodicals in Libraries in Southern California* (1968).

Specialized Checklists

Certain specialized bibliographies deserve mention as incidental sources for locating Victorian periodicals. The first two were published originally as supplements to the *Victorian Periodicals Newsletter: The Nineteenth-Century Periodical Press in Britain: A Bibliography of Modern Studies* (comp. Lionel Madden and Diana Dixon, *VPN*, 1975) and *Women and British Periodicals 1832–1867: A Bibliography* (comp. E. M. Palmegiano, *VPN*, 1976). Section A of the Madden-Dixon compilation offers "Bibliographies, Finding Lists and Reports on Bibliographical Projects," while Palmegiano's provides invaluable information on the location of every periodical listed in Section 1, "Check-List of British Women's Periodicals, 1832–1867." Both of these have been published subsequently in hardback (Madden-Dixon, 1976; Palmegiano, 1977).

One slender volume that contains valuable information about radical periodicals of the early part of the nineteenth century is Joel Wiener, *A Descriptive Finding List of Unstamped British Periodicals 1830–1836* (1970). Wiener has amassed a list of 559 entries, for which he has thoughtfully included symbols that indicate institutional holdings and which he assembled in many cases after personal shelf-check. He discusses his method for this on page xi of the introduction.

Microfilm and Microform

Today, more and more scholars are having to do their research in Victorian periodicals using microfilm or microform copies. The proliferation of microforms in the last three decades has led to several attempts to establish some sort of bibliographic control. The *Union List of Microfilms* was begun in 1942 by the Philadelphia Bibliographical Center and Union Library Catalogue, but was discontinued in 1961. The Library of Congress established a

Microfilming Clearing House in 1949 and eventually began publication of the *National Register of Microform Masters,* in September 1965. The purpose of this catalogue, which has continued as an annual volume, is to provide a record of titles for which master negatives are known to exist, so that the great expense of filming will not be duplicated. The 1966–68 volumes were divided between monographs and serials; the 1969 volume contained only serials; since 1970, serials and monographs have been listed together. Each entry is followed by a symbol identifying the location of the master and another symbol indicating the form, i.e., whether it produces an opaque copy or a transparency.

An excellent finding list for newspapers is *Newspapers on Microfilm* (1948–67), now published in two parts: *Newspapers in Microform: United States, 1948–1972* and *Newspapers in Microform: Foreign Countries, 1948–1972.* The United Kingdom section (pp. 178–95) is arranged according to the city in which each newspaper was published. Entries include publication history and frequency, libraries with holdings, type of microform, and the length of the run in each institution.

The diligent scholar will also find it profitable to consult the catalogues of commercial producers of microforms: *Guide to Microforms in Print* (Microcard Editions Books), a collective catalogue of offerings of more than one hundred publishers; *Serials in Microform* (University Microfilms); *Serials Bulletin* (University Microfilms); *International Microforms in Print* (Microforms Review, Inc.); and *Subject Guide to Microforms in Print* (Microcard Editions Books).

Computer Networks

Finally, attention must be called to the growing use of computers in libraries during the last ten years or so. In fact, according to Donald P. Hammer, executive secretary of the Information Science and Automation Division of the American Library Association, "Computers are no longer unusual in the field but commonplace. They are used to carry out all kinds of functions and procedures that serve both the internal needs of the library and the services to its patrons" (private correspondence).

One of these services has been development of bibliographic consortia, or "networking," as it is known in the field. Although there are many smaller operational networks developing all the time, the two major ones to which scholars may turn are (1) Ohio College Library Center, Frederick Kilgour, Director (1125 Kinnear Rd., Columbus, Ohio 43212; 614-422-8500) and (2) BALLOTS, Allen Veaner, Director (Stanford University Library, Stanford, Calif. 94305; 415-321-2300). An important new reference on this subject is the book by Susan K. Martin, *Library Networks, 1976-77* (White Plains, N.Y.: Knowledge Industry Publ., 1976).

The most obvious use of computer techniques in the context of Victorian periodicals will be eventually to make catalogues of individual libraries readily available, in economical form, for wide circulation among libraries and scholars.

IV

Biographical Resources

William H. Scheuerle
University of South Florida

In the December 1971 issue of *Victorian Periodicals Newsletter*, Michael Wolff, the founding president of the Research Society for Victorian Periodicals, the sponsoring organization of *VPN*, stated of periodical research that the "intellectual and scholarly rationale for the society's existence and the significance of its present and future work become clearer all the time. . . . It seems to me that all the various areas of research on Victorian Britain increasingly demand understanding of the context of the work or event or person being studied and that the periodicals are persistently recognized to be at least one, often the best, source for that context" (p. 33).

Those words have become prophetic, as more and more scholars interested in the England of 1824–1900 are recognizing the importance of Victorian periodicals for such research. But the task of researching the periodicals has often been a frustrating one, as other chapters in this *Guide* note. Not only is the number of Victorian periodicals monumental (as Wilkie Collins said, the Victorian age was THE age of periodicals), but the scholar encounters many other obstacles besides the one of culling through the sheer bulk of material. Totally accurate bibliographies of many of the periodicals are practically nonexistent; new periodicals seemingly sprang alive spontaneously and died just as suddenly, and the names of some continuing periodicals changed almost as quickly as their editors did; complete runs of periodicals seldom appear on many library shelves, save possibly at major research libraries, and those runs may be only of major periodicals. Topping the list of frustrations in dealing with Victorian periodicals is the prevalence of anonymous authorship during the nineteenth century.

There have been few bibliographies and other research resources to assist the scholar through this literary maze. Walter Houghton cogently summed up these difficulties when, writing about the *Wellesley Index*, he remarked that "The great Victorian journals have been neglected because, in good part, the maps which the scholar needs in order to explore such a large, uncharted territory have not been available" (*VPN*, 1968).

Numerous biographies have been published, of course, about major nineteenth-century literary figures who were also connected with periodicals, as have studies (some of which remain in dissertation form) of important individual journalists, but the majority of the nineteenth-century persons associated with periodicals do not fall into those classifications and have not—at least as yet—had book-length biographies written about them. Any student who wishes to gather biographical data regarding these persons must, therefore, rely upon other sources, the most useful of which are the collective biography volumes.

This, then, is the territory that this chapter will map: What general guides to biographical information—works of collected biography—are available to researchers of periodicals for data about specific editors, contributors, proprietors, illustrators, or other persons connected with the periodicals? And the concomitant question that must always be asked when one is dealing with reference material: How reliable and informative are those biographical resources?

The *Dictionary of National Biography*

The major source for biographical information on British persons associated with Victorian periodicals between 1824 and 1900 is the invaluable *Dictionary of National Biography (DNB)*. Originally published by Smith, Elder & Co. between 1885 and 1900 and edited by Sir Leslie Stephen and Sir Sidney Lee, this massive work consists of sixty-three volumes (with approximately 29,900 entries). Three additional volumes published in 1901 include lives of "distinguished persons who died at too late a date to be included in the original work" and "accidental omissions from previously published volumes." The *DNB* has since been reprinted in twenty-two volumes (including the original supplements) by the Oxford University Press (first in 1921–22). Further supplements extending past the original 1900 cutoff date continue to be issued, usually at ten-year intervals, the last being 1960. With entries ranging from short paragraphs to several pages, the *DNB* attempts to include names of "all men and women of British or Irish race who have achieved any reasonable measure of distinction in any walk of life." Because of this inclusiveness, students of Victorian periodicals should start with this indispensable reference and check not only the biographical data but also the additional bibliographical sources that are usually listed at the end of each entry.

The two-volume *Dictionary of National Biography: The Concise Dictionary* (founded by George Smith in 1882 and originally published by Smith, Elder & Co., but published by the Oxford University Press since 1920) is useful as an extended index to the main volumes of the *DNB*. In approximately one-fourteenth of the number of words that appear in the text of the *DNB*, it summarizes (with birth and death dates) the major biographies and refers the reader to the appropriate volumes and pages of the *DNB* for the detailed information. Part I publishes the biographies from the beginning to 1900; Part II, from 1901 to 1950.

A necessary addition to the *DNB* is the errata, which have been published in the *Bulletin of the [London University] Institute of Historical Research* and have been conveniently collected in the *Corrections and Additions to the Dictionary of National Biography, Cumulated from the Bulletin of the Institute of Historical Research* (1966). This cumulation covers those changes that have appeared from Volume I (1923) of the *Bulletin* to the end of Volume XXXVI (1963). Volume and page references in the cumulation are to the 1908–09 reissue of the *DNB*.

The *DNB* Project

Realizing the importance of the *DNB*, the Research Society for Victorian Periodicals began in 1968 what has come to be called the "*DNB* Project," that is, the compilation from the *DNB* of a systematic listing of anyone who died after 1824 or who was born before 1880 and who was associated with Victorian periodical publications in any capacity. The main purpose of the project is to make available an index of those Victorian periodicals and persons listed in the *DNB*. This index will be of great benefit to those scholars who are researching specific Victorian periodicals but who cannot identify every associated figure.

Under the chairmanship of William H. Scheuerle, nineteen researchers reviewed each page of the *DNB* and culled from those pages names of both major and minor nineteenth-century figures whose *DNB* entries have mentioned a connection with any Victorian periodical and whose birth or death dates fell within the critical period. That monumental task was completed in 1971, and the initial results are presently recorded on note cards at the University of South Florida, Tampa, in two indexes, with each index containing approximately 4,900 cards: one, an alphabetical listing of persons connected with Victorian periodicals, as cited by the *DNB*, and the other—and more important one—an alphabetical listing of the periodicals cross-listed with those persons.

One proof of the worth of the *DNB* Project has been the assistance that it has given to Esther and Walter Houghton, the editors of the *Wellesley Index*, and to their staff in the identification of anonymous contributors to the periodicals examined by the *Wellesley Index*. Although that aspect of the *DNB* Project was successful, to reach its total fruition for more scholars, this initial work must be built upon, as will be discussed later in this chapter.

The *DNB* researchers and the Houghtons discovered, however, the disturbing fact that the *DNB* contains pitfalls for researchers. As invaluable as the *DNB* is, *caveat investigator*: it contains a surprising amount of inaccurate information, which, for the most part, has not been corrected in the cumulative corrections. A few inaccuracies that were discovered by the Houghtons, as based upon their other research sources, and relayed to this author (example 1) and to the readers of *VPN* (1971; examples 2 and 3) will suffice to demonstrate this fact and to warn users of the *DNB* to take care:

(1) James Smetham is listed in the *DNB* as a contributor to the *Quarterly Review*, whereas he really contributed to the *London Quarterly Review*;

(2) James Roche is listed as a contributor to the *Dublin Review* "mostly under his initials." Roche died in 1851, and "JR" articles did not appear in the *Dublin Review* until 1863;

(3) George Head is assigned articles in the *Quarterly Review* that were, in fact, written by his brother, Francis Head.

The *DNB* has more fundamental shortcomings for students researching Victorian periodicals, two of which are its exclusion of biographies of many lesser-known writers who were connected with the periodicals and, at times, its exclusion of references to many of the periodicals with which a person was associated. For those reasons, and especially because of possible inaccuracies, the *DNB* entries should always be checked against biographical entries in other standard biographical sources.

In *The Art of Literary Research* (1963), Richard D. Altick states that "the chronicles of literary scholarship are studded with stories that might be entitled 'Five Little Half-Truths (or Non-Facts) and How They Grew'" (p. 18). His chapter on "The Spirit of Scholarship" delineates endless cases wherein a repeated error becomes so persuasive that it is difficult to discredit it. Scholars, therefore, must be sure of their facts and must remember that even such an invaluable source as the *DNB* may be (and often is) unreliable.

The *Modern English Biography*

The next obvious biographical research source for a student interested in a person connected with Victorian periodicals is Frederic Boase, *Modern English Biography, Containing Many Thousand Concise Memoirs of Persons Who Have Died since the Year 1850* (*MEB*) (6 vols., 1892–1921; rpt. 1965). Volumes IV, v, and vi are supplements to Volumes i, ii, and iii, respectively. Although the *MEB* is limited to "persons who have died between the years 1851 and 1900," it includes the names of persons associated with periodicals not covered by the *DNB* for these same years. As the preface to the first edition states, "many hundred notices of less known authors, artists, newspaper proprietors and journalists . . . which can be found in no other book are here recorded." This work covers approximately thirty thousand biographies. In addition, each volume contains an index "to the most important, curious and interesting facts" to be found in that volume, such as pseudonyms, lists of learned and other societies, memberships in the Royal Society, names of librarians and engravers, and initialisms.

James Ellis' article that discusses the *DNB* and the *MEB* as complementary biographical resources provides valuable reading for all scholars researching Victorian periodicals (*VPN*, 1971). A summary here of his findings will, therefore, prove useful to the scholar who is seeking guidance through the maze of periodical research. Checking all of the A's in Volume i of the *MEB* for persons connected with Victorian periodicals and then comparing that list against all of the A's culled from the corresponding section in the *DNB* by the researchers of the *DNB* Project, Ellis discovered in the *MEB* thirty-nine additional names connected with periodicals. As he has stated, some were only referred to and were "tangentially connected" with periodicals, but others were important editors, printers, compositors, and contributors to periodicals. Ellis suggests that if "one sixty-fifth of *MEB* can add thirty-nine new names to the list compiled from *DNB*, the entire *MEB* . . . might add more than 2,500."

Ellis notes two other important differences in some of the entries that he compared. Although both reference books list bibliographical sources at the conclusion of many of the entries, the *MEB* often lists sources different from those mentioned in the *DNB*. The second difference is the detail Boase gives to the place and date of births and deaths. In fact, Ellis states, "the house name or street number is often included, and, in one instance the very hour and minute of a death."

One other word may be added about the richness of the *MEB*. As Boase himself states, he "made a special study of the existence of portraits and photographs of his subjects" and gives details as to their locations.

Two entries from these two very important biographical sources are given below to compare them more clearly and to impress upon students that more than just one biographical tool must be researched.

For the first case in point, we can draw upon one of the examples that Ellis has cited and build upon his comparison: Gilbert Abbott A'Beckett (1811–56), sole or joint proprietor of numerous Victorian periodicals and one of the original staff of *Punch*. Whereas the *DNB* devotes ninety-nine lines to A'Beckett's biography, the *MEB* devotes only fifty-two, a little over half as many. But the *DNB* associates him with only eight periodicals/newspapers, while the *MEB*, connecting him with but four of these eight, relates him to another fifteen periodicals/newspapers and identifies by title of article, volume number, and date his first contribution to *Punch*. In addition, it names a series of A'Beckett's other nonperiodical publications. Importantly, the *MEB* cites five bibliographical references for him, whereas Thompson Cooper, the *DNB* contributor on A'Beckett, refers to only one source and "private information" for his knowledge. Boase's entry on A'Beckett further illustrates his interest in portraits and photographs: listed is a portrait of A'Beckett by Leech in *Punch*, 9 January 1847. Interestingly, though, Boase spells A'Beckett's middle name, Abbott, with only one *t*, whereas the other sources checked spell it with two *t*'s.

The second case in point substantiates, however, the overall usefulness of the *DNB*: John Chapman (1801–54), political writer, manufacturer, and contributor to numerous periodicals/newspapers. The *MEB* entry is short (twenty-four lines) and cites Chapman's association with only one specific journal (*Mechanic's Magazine*) but states that he was the author of "many articles" in unspecified "periodicals and newspapers." Two bibliographical sources are listed. The *DNB*, on the other hand, has an entry of 158 lines, cites the same journal but adds nine other periodicals/newspapers, including the *Westminster Review, Times*, and *Morning Advertiser*, and identifies eight of his "many articles" by specifying their titles, dates, and places of publication. His life as manufacturer and political writer is detailed, as are the cause of his death and his unfinished journalistic venture at that time. The number of bibliographical sources at the end of the entry represents a substantial increase over that of the *MEB* entry.

Allibone's *Critical Dictionary*

As for other collected biography, occasional biographical assistance, mainly for confirmation of data, may also be provided by S. Austin Allibone, *A Critical Dictionary of English Literature and British and American Authors* (1858–71; rpt. 1965). The title page outlines Allibone's intent to deal with both the "Living and Deceased . . . from the earliest accounts to the latter half of the nineteenth century." The three original volumes, with 46,000 articles, were supplemented by two additional volumes in 1891 by John Foster Kirk (rpt. 1965) that cover approximately the same period but update articles in the original first three volumes. These two supplements contain 37,000 articles. Usually the entries are short. A'Beckett's, for example, is only thirteen lines, and Chapman's is particularly limited in information: "CHAPMAN, JOHN. The Cotton and Commerce of India Considered, Lon., 1851, 8 vo. Various articles in the London quarterlies." Also noticeably absent in many of the entries are birth and death dates.

Two useful aspects of Allibone's critical dictionary are its excerpts from periodical reviews of literary works and its indexes at the end of Volume III. Forty different indexes, consisting of several hundred subindexes, are listed under the main index of "Essayists."

Other General Biographical Dictionaries

Another biographical source is *Men and Women of the Time: A Dictionary of Contemporaries*. Originally published from 1852 to 1887 as *Men of the Time: or Sketches of Living Notables*, it was retitled *Men and Women of the Time* (*MWT*) in 1891. The most useful volume for researchers of Victorian periodicals is the 1899 (fifteenth) edition, with approximately 3,400 main biographies, of which 1,560 are new to that edition, and a supplement of approximately 3,300 entries that lists not only the names of persons who had died but their birth and death dates and the edition of *MWT* in which their biographies had appeared, beginning with the fifth edition (1862). Victor G. Plarr, editor of the fifteenth edition, also included an expanded list of assumed names, a short appendix at the end of the book that contains lives omitted in the body of the work, and a classified index of occupations and professions: "Journalists, including Editors" is one. In 1901, *MWT* was incorporated into *Who's Who*, a dictionary first published by Adam and Charles Black (London) in 1849.

The annual *Who's Who* itself may not be too useful for a scholar who is interested in minor Victorian personalities or who needs to have complete biographical information on a figure. When first published, *Who's Who* consisted of a mere listing of names of very prominent living persons. It was not until 1897 that this annual started to include skeletal biographical summaries. This source, however, may be useful as one to confirm dates and lineage.

Who Was Who is a companion to *Who's Who* and is also devoted to brief biographies of prominent persons, in this case, deceased ones. The first edition, published in 1920, contains the final entries for those who had been listed in an earlier edition of *Who's Who* and had died between 1897 and 1915. Although some of the entries are updated, for the most part they are as they last appeared in *Who's Who*, with the date of death added. Publications are listed. Two later editions of *Who Was Who* that may be useful are those covering the years 1916 to 1928 and 1929 to 1940, published in 1929 and 1941, respectively.

Another "Who's Who" type of book that may assist scholars dealing with major Victorian figures who contributed to periodicals is the recently published *Who's Who in History* by G. R. R. Treasure (1974). The fifth volume in a series that has traced the portrait of the ages from the Roman and medieval periods, this new volume covers the period 1787 to 1837. Since the plan of each volume is to portray the age under consideration, the traditional alphabetical sequence of names is not followed; a loose chronological sequence of biographical essays has been adopted instead. For this reason, the index at the end of the volume is indispensable. Volume v contains approximately 160 biographical essays.

Stanley J. Kunitz and Howard Haycraft, *British Authors of the Nineteenth Century* (1936) contains approximately one thousand biographies of important deceased authors, in sketches that vary from 100 to 2,500 words. This source gives preference to writers of belles lettres, but it includes entries on other eminent figures. Bibliographies appear at the end of most of the entries and supplement and update those in the *DNB* and the *MEB*. A major difference between this source and others is its informal—almost chatty—style of writing (the contributors, in fact, had been encouraged not "to cultivate the bristling encyclopedic style") and its inclusion of 350 portraits of the chosen authors (including one, for example, of Gilbert Abbott A'Beckett).

The collected biographies described above are the basic ones for research of biographical information on persons associated with periodical publications. Others, of course, exist, but they usually duplicate the information on major figures that is collected in the basic biographies. For convenience, however, two works readily available in most libraries should be listed. *People of the Period* (ed. A. T. C. Pratt, 1897), is a two-volume source containing short biographies on approximately six thousand living persons. The second, T. H. Ward, *Men of the Reign* (1885), provides information on approximately three thousand "eminent persons of British and Colonial Birth who have died during the reign of Queen Victoria." As stated in its preface, many of the entries are reprinted from the various editions of *Men of the Time*.

Encyclopedias

Nineteenth- or early twentieth-century encyclopedias may also furnish biographical information on major figures. The *Encyclopaedia Britannica* is, of course, the most important one. Of the various editions of the *Britannica*, the eleventh (1910–11) is the most scholarly and useful, emphasizing as it does belle lettres and humanities. It was published in twenty-nine volumes, the last being an index. (The twelfth edition, 1921–22, is the republished eleventh edition, with three new volumes "dealing with events and developments of the period 1910 to 1921 inclusive.") Earlier editions of the *Britannica* useful for the period

1824–1900 are the seventh (1830–42), in twenty-one volumes; the eighth (1853–60), in twenty-two volumes; the ninth (1875–89), in twenty-five volumes; and the tenth (1902–03), which is a reprint of the ninth, with eleven supplementary volumes. It is important to remember that the *Britannica* does not include biographies of living persons and that its inclusion of Victorians associated with periodicals is selective. A biography of John Chapman, for example, does not appear in the eleventh edition.

A second encyclopedia/dictionary of value is *Chambers's Biographical Dictionary*. Originally published in the nineteenth century (1897) with approximately eleven thousand biographies, the *Dictionary* has been reprinted often. For convenience, a scholar of Victorian periodicals may wish to utilize one of the revised and enlarged modern editions (1961 or 1969, for example). This dictionary aims at "a brevity which excludes everything which is redundant and nothing that is significant."

Obituaries

Besides volumes of collective biography and encyclopedias/dictionaries, additional biographical data are available in the obituary sections in newspapers or, more specifically, in the *Times* (London). The essential guide to that source is *Palmer's Index to the [London] "Times" Newspaper* (1868–1943), which initially covered the period from 1790. Note that the obituary announcements are listed under "Deaths" and that the *Index* is divided into seasonal quarters: Jan.–Mar., Apr.–Jun., Jul.–Sept., and Oct.–Dec. Unless one knows the exact month of the death, one must investigate the "Deaths" notices in all four sections of the appropriate year. Collected editions of the obituaries of important persons from the *Times* are reprinted in *Eminent Persons: Biographies Reprinted from "The Times,"* first published in 1892.

Another source for obituaries of prominent persons is *The Annual Register: A Review of Public Events at Home and Abroad*, beginning with the year 1758 (1761–). Each obituary is a lengthy summary—sometimes extended over several pages—of the person's life similar to those summaries found in the collective biography. Thackeray's, for example, runs 215 double-columned lines.

Diaries and Autobiographies

It is worthwhile for a student interested in this period to be familiar with three references on nineteenth-century diaries and autobiographies. The first is William Matthews, *British Diaries: An Annotated Bibliography of British Diaries Written between 1442–1942* (1950). Basically a bibliography, this volume also lists biographical information, in addition to summarizing the diary, noting its publication date and place or, if not published, its location. The work is arranged chronologically but contains an author-index.

A companion to Matthews' book is John Stuart Batts's recently published *British Manuscript Diaries of the Nineteenth Century: An Annotated Listing* (1976). This listing follows the same format as Matthews' but deals only with unpublished diaries of the Victorian period, those that were started after 1800. In addition to the author-index, there is a subject-index, which concentrates upon places, people, professions, and events. Though not comprehensive, this index suggests "the range of interests to be found in nineteenth-century diaries."

Related to the above two diary references is William Matthews, *British Autobiographies: An Annotated Bibliography of British Autobiographies Published or Written before 1951* (1955; rpt. 1968). The main section of this book is an alphabetical listing by author, citing titles of autobiographies and general descriptions of the works. The index is arranged under such topics as professions, places and regions, wars, reminiscences. The index entries are heavily cross-listed.

Specialized Biographical Sources

The research sources described below are directed toward more specific classes of persons, based either on social rank or on place of education, but they may prove to be helpful either in locating new information or in confirming dates.

Although the majority of the Victorian periodicals were not edited, illustrated, or written by persons of titled rank, a researcher needs to know standard works on peerage and landed gentry. The important volumes are *Burke's Peerage, Baronetage and Knightage,* first published in 1826; *Burke's Landed Gentry,* first published in three volumes (1833–35); *Debrett's Peerage, Baronetage, Knightage, and Companionage,* first published in 1803; *Kelly's Handbook to the Titled, Landed and Official Classes,* first published in 1880; and George Edward Cokayne, *Complete Peerage of England, Scotland, Ireland, Great Britain and the United Kingdom, Extant, Extinct, or Dormant,* published between 1887 and 1898 in eight volumes. The Honorable Vicary Gibbs issued a new edition of Cokayne's work in fourteen volumes, beginning in 1910. These sources are particularly valuable for tracing a familial history.

For information on family crests a major reference is *Fairbairn's Crests of the Families of Great Britain and Ireland,* originally published in two volumes in the late nineteenth century by Thomas C. Jack, Edinburgh, Scotland. In 1968, Charles E. Tuttle Co. published a one-volume consolidation of text and plates, as revised by Laurence Butters. That edition is divided into six parts: an alphabetical listing of the family name, with a description of the crest; a glossary of heraldic terms; a translation of family mottoes; plates of the crests; and a key to the crest plates.

For nineteenth-century figures who attended Oxford or Cambridge, the scholar can check Joseph Foster, *Alumni Oxonienses* (1887–92), and John Venn and J. A. Venn, *Alumni Cantabrigienses* (1922–54). The subtitle of Foster's eight-volume book delineates clearly the contents of the brief entries: *The Members of the University of Oxford 1500–1886, Their Parentage, Birthplace, and Year of Birth, with a Record of Their Degrees.* For those persons who died during the period, there are death dates and, at times, references to their occupations. Occasionally the student finds references to supplementary sources. Venn & Venn's ten-volume biographical listing of "all known students, Graduates and Holders of Office at the University of Cambridge from the earliest times to 1900" is divided into two parts: Part I (4 vols.,

1921–27) contains the listing of students up to 1751 and Part II (6 vols., 1940–54), from 1752 to 1900. The entries in this reference are usually longer and more informative than those in *Alumni Oxonienses* and many quote supplementary sources.

Two other more limited references to scientists and engineers who may have written for Victorian periodicals should be noted, even though this chapter is not directed to reference sources dealing with specific professions and occupations. But since the following two books concentrate either in part or entirely on the nineteenth century, both in Britain and the United States, they may be useful for information on scientific and engineering journals.

The first is E. Scott Barr, *An Index to the Biographical Fragments in Unspecialized Scientific Journals* (1973). Essentially, this book serves as a means to locate biographical information and contemporary comments concerning distinguished scientists published in seven journals: *American Journal of Science* (1818–1920), *Proceedings of the Edinburgh Royal Society* (1832–1920), *Proceedings of the [London] Royal Society* (1800–1933), *Nature* (1869–1918), *Popular Science Monthly* (1872–1915), *Philosophical Magazine* (1798–1902), and *Science* (1883–1919). This index covers approximately 7,700 individuals, providing about 15,000 citations and about 1,500 portrait locations.

The second is S. P. Bell, *A Biographical Index of British Engineers in the 19th Century* (1975). This work is similar in format to Barr's, although it indexes different journals and covers different persons. Bell has indexed approximately 3,500 British engineers' obituaries that appeared in British engineering journals before 1901.

The student of Victorian periodicals, in searching for information on a particular person, would be wise to check the general bibliographies of biography for additional sources outside of the more standard sources mentioned above and the bibliographies cited in those sources. The most comprehensive is R. B. Slocum, *Biographical Dictionaries and Related Works* (1967). Although Slocum's

concern in this bibliography is primarily the biographical dictionary, closely related materials have not been neglected—

bio-bibliographies; collection of epitaphs; those genealogical works that have great biographical value; dictionaries of anonyms and pseudonyms, portrait volumes (hopefully accompanied by biographical sketches); historical and specialized subject dictionaries; government and legislative manuals that include substantial biographical material; bibliographies of individual and collective biography; biographical indexes; and selected portrait catalogs. (Preface, pp. ix–x)

It does, however, exclude general encyclopedias. This useful book is divided into three main sections: Universal Biography, National or Area Biography, and Biography by Vocation. Concomitantly, there are three indexes: Author, Title, and Subject. A 1972 supplement was issued, containing 3,400 new entries. It is important to remember that Slocum's emphasis is on the research sources, not on biographical information.

Second in importance to Slocum's work is Phyllis M. Riches, *An Analytical Bibliography of Universal Collected Biography* (1934). Unlike Slocum's, this work concentrates on indexing mainly biographical dictionaries, published, as the subtitle states, "in the English Tongue in Great Britain and Ireland, America and the British Dominions." The book is divided into two parts. The first is an alphabetical listing of persons, noting birth and death dates, if possible, and a "short description, such as 'Poet' or 'Statesman.'" Included is a mention of the books in which short biographies appear. The second part is a limited evaluative bibliography of the cited works. Like Slocum's bibliography, this reference book contains three indexes: a chronological list of persons dealt with, arranged according to centuries; a comparable index, arranged alphabetically under professions or trades; and an author and subject bibliography of biographical dictionaries.

The title of Albert M. Hyamson's *A Dictionary of Universal Biography of All Ages and of All People* (1916; rev. 1951) delineates accurately the wide scope of this resource. The prime objective of this bibliography is to include as many names as possible. As Hyamson himself states in the preface, he "never hesitated to sacrifice details to the exigencies of space, so that room might be found for additional names." Although his objective of trying to have "one person one line" is basically followed, he includes the nationality, country of adoption, and profession of the person in each entry, plus birth and death years, when possible. In some instances, and especially in the case of writers, he mentions the principal work or works. Gilbert Abbott A'Beckett, for example, is described as "Eng. Humorous wr., 'The Comic History of England,' 1811–1856." Only two references are cited: *DNB* and the *Encyclopaedia Britannica*. This bibliography is very limited in its sources.

The first edition of Hefling and Richards, *Index to Contemporary Biography and Criticism* appeared in 1929 with an index to 201 persons whose "birth(s) occurred around the year 1850 or later." Helen Hefling and Jessie W. Dyde issued a revised edition in 1934 and expanded the indexes to 417 persons. Part I is a key to the bibliographical sources, and Part II is the Index itself. This reference book guides the student to many more sources than does Hyamson's.

Biography Index: A Cumulative Index to Biographical Material in Books and Magazines (1946–), published quarterly, may be used as a guide to twentieth-century biographical material on nineteenth-century figures. The material indexed includes selected periodicals, "current books of individual and collective biographies, and incidental biographical material in otherwise non-biographical books, . . . obituaries, collections of letters, diaries, memoirs and bibliographies." The main section of this source lists the names alphabetically, usually prints birth and death dates and occupation, and cites articles and books published during the quarter under consideration. Following this main section is a list of the persons, organized by profession or occupation.

Efforts toward a Comprehensive Biographical Source

Earlier in this chapter, the *DNB* Project and the need to build upon that initial compilation were discussed. Because the members of the Research Society for Victorian Periodicals realized not only the inaccuracies in the *DNB* but also the possible inaccuracies produced by the researchers of the project in the tedious task of researching and recording their data, the project was not rushed into print. The data needed to be both checked and expanded. The first task is presently being undertaken. The index cards are in the process of being rechecked against the *DNB* entries for possible omission or misnaming of periodicals listed on the biographical cards.

Elizabeth A. Daniels of Vassar College has reported on Phase ii of the project, which has been renamed "The Directory of Victorian Journalists" (*VPN*, 1972). The six volumes of the *MEB* were researched in the same manner as the *DNB*, and the research is on file at the University of South Florida. As expected, the researchers uncovered discrepancies between the two sources in the spelling of names and in data giving street addresses, date of birth, and place of death.

Despite the completion of the initial *MEB* research, much work still needs to be accomplished. Index cards need to be made and alphabetized, and the two sets of data (*DNB* and *MEB*) should be amalgamated into combined indexes, like those set up for the *DNB*. These data should then be supplemented by comparable research in—at least—*MWT*, Allibone, and other collected biographies. This detailed task will require many researchers capable of patience and precision. The end product, however, will be worthwhile. It will be the most complete file of persons associated with Victorian periodical publications in any capacity who died after 1824 or who were born before 1880. With this major yet meager beginning, avenues of research open. Based upon this file, lists of publishers, writers, illustrators, contributors, etc., and bibliographical sources could be readily available to scholars of Victorian periodicals who are researching the periodicals per se, not just specific persons, and who require listings of persons associated with those specific periodicals. Discrepancies in biographical data would be noted and possibly eventually resolved. Perhaps, then, the "great Victorian journals" will no longer be quite the "large, uncharted territory" that they have been.

V

General Histories of the Press

Joanne Shattock

Victorian Studies Centre
University of Leicester

To the student unfamiliar with the vast scope of Victorian periodical literature, the ideal resource would be a gigantic com-
pendium, a general history of the nineteenth-century press that
would outline the various sections of this enormous range of
source materials and would act, as it were, as a kind of map. Such
a general history would distinguish the multiplicity of newspapers
—dailies, Sundays, weeklies, metropolitan and provincial—indicating their affiliations, religious or political, if any. It would ear-
mark the essentially "literary" periodicals, which contain the
bulk of reviews of current literature, creative and otherwise. It
would identify magazines designed for family consumption. It
would attempt to describe the popular press, the gigantic industry
devoted to the new Victorian reading public. It would deal with
the radical press, the newspapers that defied the stamp acts, were
overtly political and aimed at the working man, and, later in the
century, with the labor press in general. Other sections might deal
with specialist periodicals, children's magazines, theatrical journalism, women's magazines, comics, art journals, and the enormous religious press.

With such a history the scholar intent on tracing the fluctuating
reputation of a particular poet or novelist, or attempting to
analyze Victorian attitudes to children or to the family, could be

given some idea of where to begin, some notion of a range of periodicals that might prove helpful. The student of women's trade unions, the divorce question, the controversies over *Essays and Reviews* or infant baptism, or the anti-corn-law movement would gain at least an initial impression of the area into which his researches might lead him, an impression not so easily gained simply from a list of titles.

Such a history, needless to say, does not exist nor is likely to come into being. The material is simply too vast and too amorphous to be categorized. The novice, then, is left with a series of halfway houses, general histories of portions of the Victorian press, some Victorian in origin, some modern, some in volume form, others tucked away in obscure articles, some extremely useful, others of dubious value. This chapter will deal first with bibliographies of histories of the press; second, with "literary" periodicals; third, with newspapers; fourth, with the popular press; and finally, with more specialized studies.

Bibliographies

It is ironic that in an area so poorly served by the end product, bibliographies of general histories of the press are at once thorough, comprehensive, and up-to-date.

The first that should be mentioned is the one contained in Volume III of the *Cambridge Bibliography of English Literature* (1940). The subsection "Newpapers and Magazines" of the general section on "Critical and Miscellaneous Prose" contains a bibliography of "The General History of the Press." This list has been brought up to date and extensively revised by Henry and Sheila Rosenberg's entry in Volume III, Section XV, of the *New Cambridge Bibliography of English Literature* (1969), "Newspapers and Magazines." Both of these sections contain copious references to nineteenth-century accounts of the press, or sections of it, by journalists and others, published either in book form or in contemporary periodicals, as well as to important modern sources.

For twentieth-century studies, the most comprehensive listing is Lionel Madden and Diana Dixon's *The Nineteenth-Century*

Periodical Press in Britain: A Bibliography of Modern Studies 1901–1971 (Supp. to *VPN*, 1975; rpt. 1976), Section B of which is devoted to "General History of Periodicals and Newspapers." The material is complete to 1971, after which the best supplement is the annual "Victorian Periodicals: A Checklist of Scholarship and Criticism" (ed. J. Don Vann and Kenneth Mews in the Dec. issue of *VPN*). This was inaugurated in 1973 (covering work in 1971–72), thus taking up where the Madden-Dixon list left off. Because of its still modest proportions the checklist is not subdivided, but it does include general surveys of the press as well as any works that make extensive use of Victorian periodicals.

One additional bibliography worth mentioning is Carl L. Cannon, *Journalism: A Bibliography* (1924), which has useful sections on "Periodicals," "The Liberty of the Press," "Religious Journalism," and "Newspapers as Historical Sources." Much of the material is on the American press, but the individual sections frequently contain useful items not mentioned elsewhere.

Literary Periodicals

The standard survey of literary periodicals is still Walter Graham's *English Literary Periodicals* (1930; rpt. 1966). The date of publication is at once a testimony to the book's enduring usefulness—of necessity—and a sad reflection of the need for an up-to-date survey of the reviewing scene. Graham wrote long before the real resurgence of interest in the Victorian press, before projects like the *Wellesley Index* had even been conceived, and before many major studies of individual periodicals had been undertaken. His is indeed a pioneering work, and for the most part he gives a competent survey of English literary periodicals from the seventeenth century to the early twentieth.

In describing periodicals he makes the historical distinction between the magazine, a miscellany of essays, poetry, learned articles, summaries of news, obituaries, illustrations, registers of books, and even puzzles, designed both to instruct and to entertain; and the review, which developed initially from a series of abstracts of published works, through an abstract-with-comments, eventually to a series of critical reviews containing long extracts from published works, the form that the early quarterlies adopted. But because he adheres to this distinction throughout, his account of the development of nineteenth-century literary periodicals, which occupies less than half of the book, becomes somewhat distorted. The reviews, like the *Edinburgh*, the *Quarterly*, the *Fortnightly*, the *Contemporary*, the *Nineteenth Century*, the *National*, and even the *Yellow Book*, are dealt with separately from the magazines, like *Blackwood's*, the *New Monthly*, the *London Magazine*, the *Monthly Repository*, *Bentley's Miscellany*, the *Cornhill*, and *Macmillan's*. The weeklies, too, have their own chapter, ranging from the *Examiner* and *Literary Gazette*, through the *Athenaeum*, the *Spectator*, *Chambers' Edinburgh Journal*, *Notes and Queries*, the *Saturday Review*, and the *Academy*. Most of the major titles are dealt with, then, but one gets a somewhat confusing picture of the sequence of events and the important changes in the nature and style of literary reviewing.

Graham provides an accurate, if curiously constructed, skeleton, but the detail is sparse and occasionally inaccurate. He is best, not surprisingly, on the early period, the Romantic movement and afterward, and on important periodicals like the *Fortnightly* and the *Cornhill*, whose illustrious editors and contributors have for a long time been well known. He is woefully inadequate, however, on the second generation of quarterlies, those founded in the 1830s and 1840s. He does have useful sections on theatrical periodicals and on humorous magazines.

Graham, then, is a starting point, but little more. Another work of the same period, Amy Cruse's *The Englishman and His Books in the Early Nineteenth Century* (1930), contains a short chapter on "Periodicals and Their Readers," which gives a perfunctory run-through of the major periodicals in the early decades of the nineteenth century but draws on little specialist information. Far more useful is a much earlier book, Mrs. Oliphant's *The Victorian Age of English Literature*, which she wrote with F. R. Oliphant (2 vols., 1892). The second chapter, on periodical literature, is a thorough survey of reviewing in the early years and deals with both major and minor publications and the personalities involved with them. A later chapter specifically devoted to newspapers and periodicals provides a wide-ranging survey of the publications of the middle and latter decades, beginning with the *Fortnightly*, the *Contemporary*, and the *National Review* of 1883, and moving from there to the monthly magazines, art periodicals, morning and evening newspapers, both metropolitan and provincial, the weeklies, the religious press, society journals, comic journalism, and the illustrated papers. Another useful survey, of more modest proportions and more recent date, is R. G. Cox's chapter on "Reviews and Magazines" in *From Dickens to Hardy*, the sixth volume of the *Pelican Guide to English Literature* (1958), in which he succinctly describes the evolution of nineteenth-century literary periodicals, a "vast nursery," as he terms it, for the production of English literature.

As surveys are rare, a detailed picture of Victorian reviewing practices can also be gathered from several works that approach the subject indirectly. John Gross's *The Rise and Fall of the Man of Letters: Aspects of English Literary Life since 1800* (1969), is, as the title suggests, concerned with eminently literary figures, but through this polished and very readable book one gets a concrete picture of the *Edinburgh* under Francis Jeffrey, *Blackwood's* with John Gibson Lockhart and John Wilson, *Fraser's* with Maginn and Thackeray, and in the later period, of the *Saturday* reviewers at work, the *Fortnightly* under John Morley, the *Spectator* and Richard Holt Hutton, and the *Cornhill* under Leslie Stephen. In a still later period he deals with enterprises like the *Bookman* under Robertson Nicoll; with W. E. Henley and his *Magazine of Art*, the *New Review*, and the *Scots*, and later *National Observer*; and with the industrious Clement Shorter, editor of the *Illustrated London News*, the *Sketch*, the *English Illustrated Magazine*, the *Album*, and the *Pick-Me-Up*, and later founder of the *Sphere*. Gross's book is not just a series of often very acute essays on men of letters but a good portrait of the changing world of nineteenth-century journalism, from the rowdy days of the *Edinburgh* and *Blackwood's* to the more sedate milieu of the "Higher Journalism" and "The Bookmen," as his chapter titles refer to them.

A view of Victorian periodical publication can also be gained indirectly through several very different kinds of works. Neither Richard Stang's *The Theory of the Novel in England 1850–1870* (1959) nor Kenneth Graham's *English Criticism of the Novel*

1865–1900 (1965) is directly concerned with periodicals but rather with theories of the novel reflected in contemporary criticism. But both present a panorama of the weeklies, quarterlies, and monthlies whose main preoccupations were literary reviewing. Also useful in the same way are E. F. Shannon's *Tennyson and the Reviewers 1827–1851* (1952), George Ford's *Dickens and His Readers: Aspects of Novel Criticism since 1836* (1955), Michael Wolff's essay "Victorian Reviewers and Cultural Responsibility," in *1859: Entering an Age of Crisis* (ed. P. Appleman, W. A. Madden, and M. Wolff, 1959), and Isobel Armstrong's *Victorian Scrutinies: Reviews of Poetry 1830–1870* (1972). The Critical Heritage Series, published by Routledge and Kegan Paul, under the general editorship of B. C. Southam, has within the last ten years made available to most libraries a vast number of nineteenth-century reviews of major Victorian and other authors. In all of these volumes, each of which is devoted to a single author, the sections on nineteenth-century criticism are extensive, and although reviews are rarely printed in full, the selections provide both a sampling of critical style and method and a bird's-eye view of the periodicals most continuously engaged in literary reviewing throughout the century. To date, Victorian writers to whom volumes are devoted include Arnold, the Brontës, Browning, Carlyle, Clough, Collins, Dickens, George Eliot, Gissing, Hardy, Meredith, Swinburne, Tennyson, Thackeray, Trollope, and Wilde.

Yet another view of English periodical publication is the one from across the Atlantic. Clarence Gohdes, in his chapter on "The Periodicals" in *American Literature in Nineteenth-Century England* (1944), gives an interesting perspective from the midcentury on, showing which English periodicals Americans read, to which ones they contributed, and which they chose to pirate. On the last subject, James J. Barnes, in his *Authors, Publishers, and Politicians: The Quest for an Anglo-American Copyright Agreement 1815–1854* (1974), devotes a chapter to the intricacies of pirating periodicals and the alternative arrangements English and American publishers developed.

Many nineteenth-century periodicals from time to time surveyed the newspaper and periodical press, with varying degrees of accuracy and usefulness. One particular series, though, is worth

noting: Francis Espinasse's six articles, written under the pseudonym of Herodotus Smith, on "The Periodical and Newspaper
Press" in *The Critic: Journal of British and Foreign Literature
and the Arts* (1851–52). The articles give detailed accounts of
many of the literary periodicals of the period and their contributors.

The Newspaper Press

GENERAL

General histories of the newspapers of the Victorian period,
unlike those of literary periodicals, are not difficult to find. Many
were written before 1900, as journalists, editors, and other news-
papermen felt compelled, not surprisingly, to assess the century's
achievements, to record old triumphs, to evaluate competitors,
and to indulge in journalistic gossip. For this reason many of the
works, despite their authoritative titles, are suspect. Some are in
the form of rambling reminiscences, others are frankly political,
and few can profess to scholarly accuracy. Yet in some cases they
contain information otherwise unobtainable. Periodicals too had
a penchant for articles surveying the contemporary press. Here
again one must take note of the source in assessing the accuracy of
the information.

The best starting point for surveying the Victorian press is
probably E. E. Kellett's essay "The Press," in Volume II of *Early
Victorian England 1830–1865* (ed. G. M. Young, 1934). Kellett
gives a thorough description of the newspaper press, both metropolitan and provincial, outlining important background material like the "taxes on knowledge," the development of
parliamentary reporting, and the emergence of the war cor-
respondent. He interprets his brief widely, for the essay is, in
effect, a survey of all aspects of the press and includes sections on
"improving literature," the popular press, family magazines, and
the religious press. He deals too with magazines, including *Bentley's Miscellany, Household Words, Chambers' Journal, Fraser's,
Tait's,* and *Blackwood's.* He includes sections on the weeklies, like
the *Saturday,* the *Economist,* the *Athenaeum,* and *Punch.* Kellett's essay, on the face of it, might appear to be the ideal general

history mentioned at the beginning of this chapter were it not for
the fact that, once he has left the newspaper press proper, his
survey of the remainder of periodicals is arbitrary, in both selection and organization. He moves from the popular press to literary magazines to family reading, digressing along the way on
family reading habits, American pirating of English books, and
the ethos of self-help. The information he provides on some journals is minimal, and one is left at the end, not with an illuminating analysis of the nonnewspaper press, but with a somewhat
confusing series of titles.

A shorter but useful survey of the nineteenth-century news-
papers is J. S. P. Phillip's essay "The Growth of Journalism," in
Volume XIV of the *Cambridge History of English Literature* (ed.
A. W. Ward and A. R. Waller, 1916).

Of the nineteenth-century histories of the press probably the
best is H. R. Fox Bourne's *English Newspapers: Chapters in the
History of Journalism* (2 vols., 1887). The first volume deals with
the press prior to 1820. The second traces the rise of the dailies,
weeklies, biweeklies, and triweeklies, through the "radical revolt,"
to the emergence of what he sees as the modern press. Individual
newspapers, both major dailies and the cheap press, are given extensive attention.

James Grant's *The Newspaper Press: Its Origin, Progress, and
Present Position* (3 vols., 1871–72) is written in a more chatty
vein, although the preface professes a noble purpose: "The Press
has before it one of the most glorious Missions in which human
agencies ever were employed. Its Mission is to Enlighten, to Civ-
ilize, and to Morally Transform the World. . . . It has been my
aim to make this Work in some measure worthy of its great subject." Grant's chronological account is less impressive, however,
than some of the incidental chapters in his second volume, in
which he describes the actual establishment of a morning paper,
the functions of the staff, from the editor, subeditors, and readers
to the printer's devil. Another chapter describes the function of
the parliamentary reporter, another, that of the special cor-
respondent, and another, the life of the famous "penny-a-liners."
An additional chapter compares the daily papers of London, New
York, and Paris. Grant's third volume, published a year after the

first two, is entitled *The Metropolitan Weekly and Provincial Press*.

Two other contemporary accounts of the Victorian press that should be mentioned are Alexander Andrews' *The History of British Journalism* (2 vols., 1859), and *The Fourth Estate: Contributions towards a History of Newspapers, and of the Liberty of the Press* by F. Knight Hunt (2 vols., 1850). A useful early twentieth-century work is T. H. S. Escott's *Masters of English Journalism* (1911), which, despite its title, is essentially a history of the newspaper press. The nineteenth-century press is given detailed coverage, and there are chapters on the provincial press, the penny press, and the Irish press.

The advantages and pitfalls of using articles on the newspaper press from contemporary periodicals are best illustrated by some examples. The first, Francis Espinasse's series "The Periodical and Newspaper Press" in *The Critic* (1851–52), already referred to in this chapter, presents a useful and accurate survey. A second, "The Morning and Evening Papers" in *Fraser's Magazine* (May 1836) is completely biased in favor of conservative papers and therefore suspect in many of its assumptions. Another, on "The Religious Periodical Press" in *Fraser's* (Sept. 1838) is written along similar lines, with assertions that "religion is on the side of conservatism," that "as a newspaper becomes religious it ceases to be radical," and that "a dissenter's vote and his bible can never be stored in the same pocket." The main value of the article is in the series of titles it presents, some of them little-known provincial papers. The comments on them, however, are virtually worthless. One must therefore tread warily in dealing with the plethora of articles on "The Press" and "The Newspaper Press" and similar titles offered in the periodicals themselves. A knowledge of the author, or at least of the originating journal's affiliations, is essential.

A very substantial proportion of the study of the nineteenth-century newspaper press has been devoted to the London press. Donald Read's *Press and People 1790–1850: Opinion in Three English Cities* (1961) is a pioneering study of the provincial press at its best. The cities selected are Leeds, Manchester, and Sheffield, and Read provides an excellent overview of the establishment and workings of major provincial newspapers, choosing an appropriate political spectrum of papers from each city and describing both their policies and the famous editors and proprietors who conducted them. Read concludes that, despite their impressive local contributions, the influence of North-of-England newspapers upon national affairs was at best an indirect one.

Stanley Morison's *The English Newspaper: Some Account of the Physical Development of Journals Printed in London between 1622 and the Present Day* (1932) is, as the title suggests, a typographical history of the newspaper. Although of only specialist interest it does provide some fascinating insights into the importance of typography, such as the *Times*'s refusal to print any information on railway speculation between 1849 and 1852 in anything more prominent than an italic headline, in accordance with its policy of restraining the speculation craze, and, of a more trivial nature, the degrees of black border reserved for the deaths of various members of the royal family. The book also provides illustrations of typical pages of a range of papers, from the established dailies to the penny papers.

THE RADICAL PRESS

The radical press, the papers that defied the stamp acts in the first half of the century, have received a disproportionate amount of attention, particularly from social historians. Two main works stand out. Joel H. Wiener, in *The War of the Unstamped: The Movement to Repeal the British Newspaper Tax, 1830–1836* (1969), presents an excellent profile of the illegal penny press during these six years, their editors and proprietors, and the sophisticated techniques employed in their production and distribution. His concern is as much with the men behind the papers and the radical movement they reflected as with the papers themselves. Patricia Hollis, in *The Pauper Press: A Study in Working-Class Radicalism of the 1830s* (1970), like Wiener, sees the unstamped press as part of a wider radical movement that developed further long after the struggles over the newspaper stamp duty subsided. Her description of the contents and functions of particular papers is fuller than Wiener's, and she gives a fascinating description of the business organization of the radical press.

An earlier study, William S. Wickwar's *The Struggle for the Freedom of the Press 1819–1832* (1928), covers some of the same ground, but is more concerned with the actual legal struggle than with the newspapers themselves. Simon Maccoby, in his six-volume history of *English Radicalism* (1935–61), makes extensive use of the radical press, but the third volume, *English Radicalism 1832–1852* (1935), has a specific section devoted to "The Newspaper Press." Also relevant to this general theme is Arthur Aspinall's *Politics and the Press 1780–1850* (1949), a detailed study of attempts at governmental control of the press in the first half of the century through advertisements, offers of free circulation, and other subsidies, and of the successful efforts of the press to extricate itself from such control.

Most of the work on the political press has concentrated on the first third of the century, concluding with the reduction of the stamp duty in 1836. Stanley Harrison's less scholarly and more general study, *Poor Men's Guardians: A Record of the Struggles for a Democratic Newspaper Press, 1763–1973* (1974), carries the story further, dealing with the Chartist press and with later papers like the *Commonweal*, Keir Hardie's *The Miner*, and early Fabian journals. Writing essentially a popular history that extends to the present day, Harrison is more concerned with his theme of the struggle for the freedom of the press than with individual papers, but he does provide a chronological account for the latter half of the century. Also concerned with the later part of the Victorian period is Alan J. Lee's *The Growth of the Popular Press in England 1855–1914* (1976). Lee sees the emergence of a cheap daily press in the 1860s as not only the culmination of ideological struggles but also the result of technical and economic changes. He traces the influence of economic growth on the liberal vision of the cheap press through to the period immediately preceding the First World War.

An excellent short study of the role of the working-class political press is Stephen Coltham's "English Working Class Newspapers in 1867" (*VS*, 1969). Coltham selects five papers, all with a claim to being strictly working class—the *National Reformer*, the *Commonwealth*, the *Working Man*, the *Bee-Hive*, and the *International Courier*—and describes in detail the activities of these papers in the reform movement of 1867.

The Popular Press

The "Victorian reading public" has become a hallowed concept in the minds not only of social historians but of literary critics and historians as well. The literary merits and social significance of the literature produced for its instruction and amusement have been the subject of endless discussion and analysis over the past two decades, and the periodical press has played a not inconsiderable part in the debate. Consequently, material on cheap periodicals, those designed specifically to "amuse and instruct," as distinct from the working-class newspaper press with a deliberate political overtone, is abundant.

Raymond Williams, in an important chapter, "The Growth of the Reading Public," in *The Long Revolution* (1961), reminds us that "there is still a quite widespread failure to co-ordinate the history of the press with the economic and social history with which it must necessarily be interpreted." Several works have attempted to do just that and to describe the literature created for the new, largely urban, working-class reader. R. K. Webb's *The British Working Class Reader 1790–1848: Literary and Social Tension* (1955) deals in depth with the social and economic implications of the new literacy but also includes sections on the periodicals created during the period. Richard D. Altick, in *The English Common Reader: A Social History of the Mass Reading Public 1800–1900* (1957), devotes two chapters to "Newspapers and Periodicals," one on the period from 1800 to 1850 and a second from 1851 to 1900. J. W. Dodds, in *The Age of Paradox: A Biography of England 1841–1851* (1952), has a useful chapter, "1843 'To Amuse and Instruct,'" that surveys the popular literature available during that particular year, including the periodicals.

Two of the best surveys of cheap periodicals occur in works devoted to studies of the popular fiction of the nineteenth century. Louis James's excellent *Fiction for the Working Man 1830–1850* (1963) indirectly gives a detailed profile of the mass-produced periodicals and their entrepreneurs. Margaret Dalziel, *Popular Fiction 100 Years Ago* (1957), covers a wider field and includes religious periodicals that are not discussed by James. Finally, Q. D. Leavis' *Fiction and the Reading Public* (1932), though its concerns are far wider, has valuable insights for any student of the nineteenth-century reading public and periodical literature.

Specialized Studies

ART PERIODICALS

Nineteenth-century English art periodicals have been virtually ignored until recently, partly because they were few in number and were dwarfed, on the one hand, by their continental counterparts and, on the other, by twentieth-century giants like the *Burlington Magazine* (1903) and the *Connoisseur* (1901). However, an exhibition on "The Art Press" at the Victoria and Albert Museum in the spring of 1976, which coincided with an international conference on art periodicals by the Art Libraries Society (ARLIS), produced an important publication that went some way to remedy this neglect. *The Art Press: Two Centuries of Art Magazines*, edited by Trevor Fawcett and Clive Phillpot (1976), is, as the editors emphasize, "the first attempt to consider the art periodical as a genre and as a significant factor in the development of art and its understanding." Anthony Burton, in "Nineteenth Century Periodicals," deals with both English and European journals, beginning his survey of English periodicals with the important *Annals of the Fine Arts* (1816–20) and continuing through to Victorian publications like Samuel Carter Hall's *Art Journal* (1839) (formerly called the *Art Union*), the *Fine Arts Quarterly Review*, and others. He also includes American art journals in this useful survey. Trevor Fawcett's article "Scholarly Journals" begins with the late nineteenth century and concentrates on European publications, but it does refer back to some English titles. His second essay, on "Illustration and Design," discusses methods of illustration, from engraving and lithography to photogravure, and their influence on a number of nineteenth-century periodicals, from the *Penny Magazine* and *Punch* to more specifically art periodicals.

Happily coinciding with the Victoria and Albert's exhibition, the seventy-fifth anniversary number of the *Connoisseur* (Mar. 1976) contains a series of essays on art journals, including several on nineteenth-century publications. Michael Collins' "English Art Magazines before 1901" deals mainly with the illustrated periodicals of the 1880s and 1890s. Jeremy Maas writes on "S. C. Hall and the *Art Journal*"; Joseph T. Butler, on "Art and Antiquarian Periodicals in the United States"; and Anthony Burton concludes the series with a study of *"L'Artiste* and Some Other Magazines of European Romanticism."

WOMEN'S PERIODICALS

For some reason, the number of general histories of periodicals for women—to date, at least—has not caught up with the general interest in women studies and in the Victorian woman in particular. Only two major works have emerged. Alison Adburgham's *Women in Print: Writing Women and Women's Magazines from the Restoration to the Accession of Victoria* (1972), as the title implies, deals only with the periodicals of the first third of the century. Again, as she implies in her title, she is as much concerned with the phenomenon of women earning a living by writing and editing and their resulting social status as she is in the women's magazines themselves. She does, however, in a chapter on "Periodicals of the New Century," deal thoroughly with early periodicals and their contributors. Another chapter deals extensively with the rise of the annuals and with their female contributors, and another, on "Writing Women of the Thirties," discusses the new magazines of the 1830s and their contributors.

A more wide-ranging book is Cynthia L. White's *Women's Magazines 1693–1968* (1970), which traces the history of the women's magazine from its seventeenth-century originals and contains two sections on nineteenth-century publications, "The Origins of the Women's Press: 1693–1865" and "An Industry Is Born: 1875–1910." Both are useful in describing major publications, their proprietors, and their contributors. Both White and Adburgham, interestingly, arrive at the same conclusion, that, as the nineteenth century progressed, women's magazines became

less and less concerned with improving the mind and more ob-
sessed with domestic issues of home, family, and fashion.

CHILDREN'S PERIODICALS

Children's periodicals are another area that has received comparatively little attention, at least in survey form. Sheila A. Egoff,
in her *Children's Periodicals of the Nineteenth Century* (1951),
illustrates the range of material and provides a bibliography.
Boys' periodicals, too, a perennial preoccupation of amateur en-
thusiasts, have had little serious work done on them. E. S. Turner's *Boys Will Be Boys* (1948) deals indirectly with boys'
periodicals in a study of their most popular heroes, Sweeney
Todd, Deadwood Dick, Sexton Blake, Billy Bunter, and Dick
Barton. Not all of the material is Victorian, but a fair proportion
deals with nineteenth-century magazines. Ralph Rollington's *The
Old Boys' Books: A History of the Old Time Journals for Boys,
Their Publishers, Authors, Artists, and Editors* (1913), despite its
promising title, falls into the category of amateur reminiscences.
Rollington was himself the proprietor of four boys' journals and
writer of many stories for boys. Part II, "A Brief History of Boys'
Papers," does give a short publishing history of some titles, noting
their contents, contributors, and proprietors; a brief appendix by
"H. S." adds others. Louis James, in "Tom Brown's Imperialist
Sons" (*VS*, 1973), contributes a useful study of the penny publi-
cations of Edwin J. Brett, publisher of *Boys of England, Young
Men of Great Britain*, and *Boys of the Empire*, and of George
Emmett, whose titles included *The Young Englishman's Journal,
Young Gentlemen of Britain*, the *Young Briton*, and *Sons of
Britannia*.

COMICS

The nineteenth-century antecedents of the modern comic received little attention until the recent studies of Denis Gifford,
first in his article "The Evolution of the British Comic" (*History
Today*, 1971) and more recently in his *British Comic Catalogue
1874–1974* (1975), *Happy Days: A Century of Comics* (1975),
and *Victorian Comics* (1976).

THEATRICAL JOURNALISM

Theatrical periodicals are one of the major sources of information about the nineteenth-century theater. Yet very little has been written about them. Carl J. Stratman makes this point in the introduction to his *Bibliography of English Dramatic Periodicals 1720–1960* (1962). The introduction surveys some nineteenth-century periodicals, including provincial ones, and points out the high proportion of publications that were published outside London. A second, and revised, edition of this work was published in 1972, under the title *Britain's Theatrical Periodicals 1720–1967: A Bibliography*.

TEMPERANCE PERIODICALS

A very good example of the kind of brief study that needs to be done on specialized sections of the Victorian press is Brian Harrison's " 'A World of Which We Had No Conception': Liberalism and the Temperance Press 1830–1872" (*VS*, 1969). Harrison shows how the temperance movement, largely through its press, became an important social force, one of the many that ultimately helped to shape Gladstonian liberalism. Many of the periodicals he describes are referred to again in his *Drink and the Victorians* (1971).

THE NINETIES

While individual periodicals and, of course, authors of the nineties have been extensively studied, there has been surprisingly little work on the nineties periodical press as a whole. J. R. Tye, in an unpublished thesis, "Literary Periodicals of the Eighteen-Nineties: A Survey of the Monthly and Quarterly Magazines and Reviews" (Oxford Univ. 1971), describes in detail the range of periodicals, their publishers and printers, editors and contributors, and the recurrent literary themes that were reflected in their contents over the decade. A bibliography of nineties' titles resulting from this research has been published by the Oxford Bibliographical Society, *Periodicals of the Nineties: A Checklist of Literary Periodicals Published in the British Isles at Longer than Fortnightly Intervals* (1974).

THE RELIGIOUS PRESS

It is perhaps deceptive to single out religious periodicals, as many quarterlies and weeklies had sectarian affiliations but managed to maintain sufficient independence from their sponsoring bodies to be regarded as purely literary or family magazines. However, there are many that did not, and some inroads into this vast area have been made. L. E. Elliott-Binns, in his *Religion in the Victorian Era* (1936), has a chapter on the press that describes briefly some little-known periodicals. P. G. Scott has produced several useful contributions, including "Richard Cope Morgan, Religious Periodicals, and the Pontifex Factor" (*VPN*, 1972) and "Victorian Religious Periodicals: Fragments That Remain," in *The Materials, Sources, and Methods of Ecclesiastical History* (ed. Derek Baker, 1975). Baptist periodicals have been surveyed in Rosemary Taylor's unpublished thesis, "English Baptist Periodicals 1790–1865: A Bibliography and Survey" (M. Phil. Univ. of London 1974).

OTHER PERIODICALS

Nineteenth-century English music journals are surveyed briefly in Volume VI of *Grove's Dictionary of Music and Musicians* (5th ed., 1954). Richard A. Cosgrove, in "Victorian Legal Periodicals" (*VPN*, 1975), gives an outline of a hitherto untouched area of professional journalism. Legal periodicals are also touched on in W. M. Maxwell's *Law Publishing Then and Now: 1799–1974* (1975). University journalism, now a largely forgotten field, is described in Vernon Horace Rendell's essay "University Journalism" in Volume XIV of the *Cambridge History of English Literature* (1916).

One final source is Alvar Ellegård's *The Readership of the Periodical Press in Mid-Victorian Britain* (Göteborg, 1957). Although primarily devoted to circulation figures, this very useful pamphlet provides thumbnail sketches of numerous periodicals, indicating their readership, political or religious affiliation, if any, and other information. The periodicals are divided into "Newspapers," daily, evening, weekly, and religious; "Weekly Reviews and Newspapers of the Review Type"; "Fortnightly to Quarterly Reviews"; "Monthly Magazines"; and "Weekly Journals and Magazines Sold in Weekly Parts." Although more recent research has proved some of Ellegård's assumptions about readership and affiliation incorrect, the lists of periodicals under each heading illustrate the range available, and the accompanying notes are often the only source of information of its kind.

VI

Histories and Studies
of Individual Periodicals

Lionel Madden and Diana Dixon
College of Librarianship Wales, Aberystwyth

Primary Source Materials

Students undertaking a detailed historical or critical survey of a Victorian periodical may well find themselves faced with the extremes of either an overwhelming abundance or a severe deficiency of source materials. Before attempting an analysis of the studies already produced in this field, therefore, it may be useful to survey briefly the sources that are available to the researcher.

The basic source for the study of any periodical is, of course, the periodical itself. In addition to its normal contents it may include at certain times specifically historical information about itself. Such information is most likely to be found in anniversary issues. Examples of such special issues are cited below, especially in the last section. It is sometimes possible, too, to trace a prospectus of the periodical that will indicate the original aims of its founders and may also list the names of individuals involved in planning the periodical. Inevitably, such prospectuses are extremely ephemeral and elusive. Being issued before the formal commencement of the periodical itself, they are often not bound in with the periodical set in library collections. There is an interesting sample collection of prospectuses, acquired as examples of printed ephemera, in the John Johnson Collection in the Bodleian Library in Oxford.

In the case of obscure or short-lived periodicals, the set of the periodical itself may be, indeed, the only source material available to the student. For many periodicals, however, it will be possible to supplement knowledge derived from the periodical itself by other published and unpublished materials. The most likely sources are records of individuals associated with the periodical and records of the publishing house that published it.

Many contemporary autobiographical and biographical memoirs of Victorian proprietors, editors, and contributors have been published. These, as well as more recent studies of such individuals, may be traced through the usual bibliographical tools. Basic information on the searching of relevant bibliographies and reference works for Victorian studies is given in Lionel Madden's *How to Find Out about the Victorian Period: A Guide to Sources of Information* (1970). Guidance on specifically biographical tools is given by William H. Scheuerle in Chapter iv of this *Guide*. There are several published studies of Victorian publishing houses embodying research based on the use of the publisher's records. A good example is Royal A. Gettmann's *A Victorian Publisher: A Study of the Bentley Papers* (1960). Studies have often been issued to commemorate anniversaries in the life of the firm, such as Simon Nowell-Smith's *The House of Cassell 1848–1958* (1958).

Unpublished materials relating to individuals or publishing houses may often be traced through the records maintained by the National Register of Archives. The indexes, which may be consulted in the search room of the National Register of Archives (Quality Court, Chancery Lane, London WC2A 1HP), are primarily concerned to give information about the location of manuscripts in Britain. The Register's indexes include a subject index, an index of personal names, and a geographical index. Entry to the index of personal names is, on the whole, restricted to people of sufficient eminence to have found a place in the *Dictionary of National Biography* or *Who Was Who*. There are some interesting brief comments on the value of the National Register of Archives for students of Victorian periodicals by Roger Ellis, formerly Secretary of the Royal Commission on Historical Manuscripts (of which the Register forms part), in the *Victorian Periodicals Newsletter* (1968).

The indexes of the National Register of Archives do not include entries for the collections in the national repositories. Thus the National Library of Scotland's holdings of the papers of William Blackwood and Sons would have to be traced through the Library's own published *Catalogue of Manuscripts*, the third volume of which is entitled *Blackwood Papers 1805–1900* (1968). Manuscripts located in repositories in the United States can be sought in the *National Union Catalog of Manuscript Collections. A Guide to Archives and Manuscripts in the United States* (ed. Philip M. Hamer, 1961) is still a useful one-volume guide.

Archives of certain Victorian publishers are available in a collection entitled "The Archives of British Publishers on Microfilm" produced by Chadwyck-Healey in Britain and distributed in the United States by Somerset House. The first series is rich in Victorian material, comprising the archives of George Allen & Co., 1893–1915; George Routledge & Co., 1853–1902; the Cambridge University Press, 1696–1902; Kegan Paul, Trench, Trübner & Henry S. King, 1853–1912; Swan Sonnenschein & Co., 1878–1911; and Elkin Mathews, 1811–1938. Separate printed indexes have been published for the Allen, Swan Sonnenschein, and Kegan Paul archives, and E. S. Leedham-Green has written an introductory *Guide to the Archives of the Cambridge University Press* (1973). The second series comprises the archives of Richard Bentley & Son, 1829–98. This series is accompanied by a microfiche of Bentley's annual lists of publications, 1829–98, and a printed *Index and Guide* to the lists by Michael L. Turner (1975). The third series includes the archives of Longman, 1794–1914, and Grant Richards, 1897–1948. Both are supplied with printed indexes.

It is difficult to know with any precision how many publishers' archives are still extant. In an attempt to improve the situation and to facilitate the use of manuscript source materials generally, one of the first projects encouraged by *Victorian Periodicals Newsletter* and, later, by the Research Society for Victorian Periodicals was a checklist, or survey, of manuscript sources relevant to the study of Victorian periodicals. The idea of such a checklist was first put forward by the late H. W. McCready, and he reported on the project at intervals in the *Newsletter*. It was originally proposed that the project should be concerned both with listing manuscript resources in libraries and also with locating publishers', printers', and other records. However, in a meeting at the Victorian Periodicals Conference in New York in 1969, it was decided, realistically, that it would be impossible to compile a checklist of manuscript resources relevant to Victorian periodicals; a recommendation was made instead that the editors of *Victorian Periodicals Newsletter* should establish a regular "Manuscript Notes and Queries" section in the *Newsletter* as a means of exchanging information. Although the recommendation was adopted, it did not result in the desired flow of information from readers, and in March 1972, Scott Bennett reported on a new proposal by McCready for a register of manuscript materials relating to a limited number of writers associated with those periodicals included in the *Wellesley Index*. The first fruits of this approach were published in the form of a preliminary list by McCready (*VPN*, 1974). In the September 1974 issue, McCready published an article on "The *Quarterly Review* in 1898 and 1919, Documented from the Prothero Papers at the Royal Historical Society."

Bibliographies

There are two major bibliographies of studies of nineteenth-century periodicals. The first is a general listing of selected contemporary and modern studies. The other, while considerably more comprehensive, is confined to twentieth-century studies.

The major general list is the magisterial entry on "Newspapers and Magazines" contributed by Henry and Sheila Rosenberg in Volume III of the *New Cambridge Bibliography of English Literature* (ed. George Watson, 1969). Although indebted to the earlier list by Graham Pollard in the original *Cambridge Bibliography* (1940), the Rosenbergs' work represents a genuine revision, incorporating a considerable amount of new material as well as inevitable changes in arrangement. As the compilers pointed out in an informative short article, "Nineteenth-Century

Newspapers and Magazines in the *New CBEL"* (*VPN*, 1968), their list aims to be interdisciplinary in scope and is certainly not restricted specifically to titles of literary interest. It is therefore potentially of value to all students of the period, whether or not they are literary scholars. The bibliography has two purposes: to list a representative selection of periodicals and to note important published historical and critical studies of the nineteenth-century press generally and of specific titles. Thus, while much of the entry is inevitably devoted to the listing of titles of specific magazines and newspapers, the bibliography is also valuable for our purposes. For many of the more important and several of the minor titles it gives reading lists of published studies. In particular, there are good lists of studies of individual London and provincial newspapers of both general and special interest, monthly and quarterly magazines, school and university journals, and literary annuals.

The second important bibliography of studies of periodicals is *The Nineteenth-Century Periodical Press in Britain: A Bibliography of Modern Studies 1901–1971* (comp. Lionel Madden and Diana Dixon, supp. to *VPN*, 1975; rpt. 1976). The bibliography lists 2,632 writings that have appeared as published books, pamphlets, or articles, or as unpublished theses or manuscript studies deposited in libraries. The four sections of the work list bibliographies, general historical studies of nineteenth-century periodicals, studies of individual periodicals, and studies and memoirs of proprietors, editors, journalists, and contributors. The bibliography is based upon a personal check of items listed in previous bibliographical sources and upon personal examination of the contents of a wide range of British libraries. Items are frequently annotated to expand the title or to draw attention to points of particular value. Although it is still far from exhaustive, this work does represent the most comprehensive bibliography yet compiled of writings about nineteenth-century periodicals. It is particularly helpful in indicating the considerable historical material that is buried in anniversary issues and supplements. Planning of the bibliography was undertaken in conjunction with Henry and Sheila Rosenberg, who commenced working simultaneously to produce a complementary work listing studies published before 1901. Detailed reports on the planning and development of both projects have been published (*VPN*, 1968, 1970, 1971).

The bibliography by Madden and Dixon terminates at 1971. For publications relating to nineteenth-century periodicals since 1971 the student is well served by the "Checklist of Scholarship and Criticism" now published annually in *Victorian Periodicals Newsletter* under the editorship of J. Don Vann and Kenneth Mews. This annual bibliography lists "articles and books which deal to any large extent with Victorian periodicals." Items are briefly annotated where this is necessary to clarify the subject, and—a very useful service—important reviews are listed. The author arrangement is supplemented by indexes of names, periodical titles, and subjects. It is, therefore, easy to identify at a glance new studies of individual periodicals. It is perhaps to be regretted that the annual "Victorian Bibliography" in *Victorian Studies* did not prove sufficiently flexible in arrangement to accommodate this material in a form that would be most useful to students of periodicals. Clearly, one must have reservations about the unnecessary duplication that inevitably results from the proliferation of bibliographies within specialized fields such as Victorian studies. There is, however, no doubt that at present the *Victorian Periodicals Newsletter* annual bibliography is fulfilling a valuable service that is not available elsewhere.

The entry under "Periodical Publications" in the published *General Catalogue of Printed Books* of the British Library Reference Division (formerly the British Museum Library) is primarily a record of the Library's holdings of periodicals, arranged by place of publication. Entries for specific titles do, however, include references to significant studies, though those published in the twentieth century will normally have been incorporated in the Madden-Dixon bibliography.

Users of the *Wellesley Index to Victorian Periodicals 1824–1900* (ed. Walter E. Houghton, 1966–) will be familiar with the excellent introductions that precede the entry for each periodical. Each introduction includes a useful "Bibliographical Note" drawing attention to significant items about the periodical. Many of the bibliographical notes are written in narrative form and are frankly evaluative.

William S. Ward's *British Periodicals and Newspapers, 1789–*

1832: A Bibliography of Secondary Sources (1974) is occasionally useful for the early years of our period. Section 3 lists books and articles about individual magazines and newspapers.

Magazines

In general, serious and sustained study of individual Victorian magazines has tended to concentrate on those titles that have long been recognized by students of the period as having been particularly influential in their own age. The roll call of titles that have formed the subject of significant monographs indicates clearly enough the type of magazine that has most frequently attracted serious attention: the *Academy,* the *Athenaeum, Fraser's Magazine,* the *Saturday Review,* the *Fortnightly Review,* the *Monthly Repository,* the *Rambler,* and the like. Clearly we are here in the world of weighty and informed opinion, of wide-ranging and detailed discussion, of intense political awareness. If the titles are not always the same, the ethos is recognizably akin to the monthlies and quarterlies selected for inclusion in the *Wellesley Index.*

As was noted in the first section of this chapter, an author undertaking a study of such a magazine may be faced with an unwieldy mass of source materials. Leslie A. Marchand, in his *The* Athenaeum: *A Mirror of Victorian Culture* (1941), describes his aim as "to carve from a massive bulk of material, mainly from the magazine itself in its heyday, something like a rounded image" of the magazine. In addition to the contents of the magazine itself, students will often have available to them a wide range of autobiographical and biographical memoirs and studies of persons associated with the magazine, as well as unpublished materials. In Marchand's case, for example, he was able to draw on the memoirs of Sir Charles Dilke, John Collins Francis, and John Francis, as well as on the Dilke Papers and marked files of the *Athenaeum.*

Like Marchand, many of the authors of monographs on specific magazines have set out to give a "rounded image" of the magazine throughout the whole or part of its history by a survey of its origins and development, a study of its proprietors, editors, and leading contributors, and an analysis of its distinctive viewpoint and attitudes. So Marchand follows an outline of the history of the

Athenaeum with an account of Dilke's fight against literary puffery, an analysis of the reviewers and contributors who worked for the magazine under Dilke's editorship, and a representative cross section of literary criticism, especially of the works of major authors.

A similar atttempt at a "rounded image" is found in Francis E. Mineka's *The Dissidence of Dissent: The* Monthly Repository *1806–1838* (1944), which traces the history of the magazine from relative unimportance as a miscellaneous journal of the Unitarians to a liberal magazine of political, social, and literary importance. As Marchand's interest in the *Athenaeum* is especially concerned with the fight for independent literary criticism, so Mineka is preeminently interested in the religious, political, and social criticism of the *Monthly Repository* and in tracing its attitudes on such issues as the emancipation of women. As in several of the monographs, the author provides an appendix identifying contributors.

Among the attempts at a detailed general picture of a magazine must be mentioned a much older work, M. H. Spielmann's *The History of* Punch (1895). This very substantial volume is rich in anecdotes and illustrations. Spielmann claimed to have personally contacted hundreds of persons whom he suspected of having worked for *Punch*, and almost half the book is devoted to the identification of writers and artists who contributed to the magazine. *Punch* has, of course, inspired—and continues to inspire—many acts of piety in the form of volumes of selections from its pages, but few of its admirers have gone to such lengths in documentation as Spielmann. R. G. G. Price's *A History of Punch* (1957), although informative and entertaining, is declaredly more modest in its aims. It succeeds as an intelligent, nonscholarly sketch of *Punch*'s development, with emphasis on its history during the twentieth century.

Rather than attempting a comprehensive survey, several writers have chosen to make an intensive study of a limited period in the life of a magazine—often concentrating their attention on the opening years. Miriam M. H. Thrall's *Rebellious* Fraser's: *Nol Yorke's Magazine in the Days of Maginn, Thackeray, and Carlyle* (1934) is concerned with the first decade of the magazine, 1830–40. It includes a list of contributors that has been used by the *Wellesley Index* editor "heavily but uneasily" (because of the absence of stated evidence for most of the attributions). Thrall examines in some detail the relationship of Carlyle to the magazine and the evolution of Thackeray's work under the editorship of Maginn. Maginn's editorship is assessed with attention to the controversial aspects of his reputation.

Edwin M. Everett's *The Party of Humanity: The* Fortnightly Review *and Its Contributors, 1865–1874* (1939) also analyzes the magazine during its first ten years, discussing its success as a novel experiment in journalism and summarizing its contents during that period. Merle M. Bevington's *The* Saturday Review *1855–1868: Representative Educated Opinion in Victorian England* (1941) studies the magazine's attitudes on a wide variety of topics under its first editor, John Douglas Cook. The final chapter gives a brief summary of the magazine's subsequent history to 1938. Another notable and widely used older study of the early history of a magazine is George L. Nesbitt's *Benthamite Reviewing: The First Twelve Years of the* Westminster Review *1824–1836* (1934). Nesbitt traces the history of the periodical during its strictly Benthamite period and summarizes the opinions expressed in it.

D. Roll-Hansen's *The* Academy *1869–1879: Victorian Intellectuals in Revolt* (1957) widens the scope from the mere discussion of the magazine itself to the whole arena of intellectual history. Roll-Hansen attempts not merely to portray the development of the magazine during its first decade but, more important, to indicate the origin and nature of the crusading spirit that motivated young university liberals. A considerable portion of the book is devoted to discussion of the intellectual background of the period.

Several magazines have been the subject of celebratory studies on the occasion of anniversaries. William B. Thomas' *The Story of the* Spectator *1828–1928* (1928) discusses the editors—R. S. Rintoul, Richard Holt Hutton, Meredith Townsend, and John St. Loe Strachey—and then examines the magazine's attitudes to nineteenth-century issues and events. *The* Economist *1843–1943: A Centenary Volume* (1943) comprises a series of essays discussing aspects of the history and contents of the *Economist*.

Anthologies can provide useful introductions to the preoccupations and tone of a magazine. Some include prefatory essays. There is a good discussion of the *Nineteenth Century* by Michael Goodwin in his *Nineteenth-Century Opinion* (1951), an anthology of the first fifty years of the magazine. Fraser Harrison's *The Yellow Book: An Illustrated Quarterly: An Anthology* (1974) has a long introductory essay, though for a more detailed treatment the reader should turn to Katherine Lyon Mix's *A Study in Yellow: The* Yellow Book *and Its Contributors* (1960).

In the case of some magazines, of course, the best treatment is to be found hidden in other monographs. J. W. Robertson Scott's *The Story of the* Pall Mall Gazette (1950) includes the fullest account of the *Cornhill Magazine*. The best account of the first decade of the *Contemporary Review* is to be found in Alan W. Brown's *The Metaphysical Society* (1947). John Clive has contributed an important account of "The *Edinburgh Review*: The Life and Death of a Periodical" in *Essays in the History of Publishing in Celebration of the 250th Anniversary of the House of Longman 1724–1974* (ed. Asa Briggs, 1974).

More commonly, the standard account is contained in the biography of the founder of the publishing house or in the biographies of the magazine's most notable editors. An early example is Margaret Oliphant's *Annals of a Publishing House: William Blackwood and His Sons—Their Magazine and Friends* (1897), completed by Mrs. Gerald Porter (1898), which gives the best account of *Blackwood's Edinburgh Magazine*. More recently, Royal A. Gettmann's *A Victorian Publisher: A Study of the Bentley Papers* (1960) includes an account of *Bentley's Quarterly Review*.

Despite the efforts of scholars, a surprising number of important magazines have received no detailed study. Of the eight magazines included in the first volume of the *Wellesley Index*, six are recorded in the Bibliographical Notes as having no full-scale historical and critical study. These are the *Contemporary Review*, the *Cornhill Magazine*, the *Edinburgh Review*, the *Home and Foreign Review*, *Macmillan's Magazine*, and the *North British Review*. This last has now been exhaustively treated in E. J. Shattock's doctoral dissertation, "A Study of the *North British Review* (1844–1871): Its History, Policies, and Contributors" (Univ. of London 1973). The early history of the *Cornhill Magazine* has been the subject of a short monograph by Spencer L. Eddy, *The Founding of the* Cornhill Magazine (1970). Eddy also presented "A History of the Editorship of the *Cornhill Magazine* 1860–96" as his doctoral dissertation (Rutgers Univ. 1970). Of the other magazines, *Blackwood's Edinburgh Magazine* is most fully treated in Margaret Oliphant's *Annals of a Publishing House,* noted above, while the *Quarterly Review* has been the subject of two full-length studies. The early years, which fall outside our period, are discussed in the introduction to Hill and Helen Chadwick Shine's *The* Quarterly Review *under Gifford: Identification of Contributors 1809–24* (1949). Walter J. Graham, in *Tory Criticism in the* Quarterly Review *1809–53* (1921), deals with a more specific aspect of the magazine.

A check of the second volume of the *Wellesley Index* reinforces the point. Of the twelve magazines indexed, only one has been the subject of a full-length published study. Josef L. Altholz' *The Liberal Catholic Movement in England: The* Rambler *and Its Contributors 1848–64* (1962) provides the detailed scholarly history of that magazine, with a chapter on its short-lived successor, the *Home and Foreign Review.* Two other magazines—the *Fortnightly Review* and *Fraser's Magazine*—have received partial attention in the works by Everett and Thrall noted above. The *Foreign Quarterly Review* is studied at length in Eileen M. Curran's doctoral dissertation, "The *Foreign Quarterly Review* (1827–1846): A British Interpretation of Modern European Literature" (Cornell Univ. 1958). One aspect of the *National Review* is studied in Robert M. Christian's doctoral dissertation "Leo Maxse and the *National Review*: A Study in the Periodical Press and British Foreign Policy 1893–1914" (Univ. of Virginia 1940). Another doctoral dissertation provides a brief historical introduction to the *Oxford and Cambridge Magazine*; this is Walter K. Gordon's "A Critical Selected Edition of William Morris's *Oxford and Cambridge Magazine* (1856)" (Univ. of Pennsylvania 1960). Leo J. Walsh's doctoral dissertation, "William Ward and the *Dublin Review*" (Columbia Univ. 1962) includes a historical survey of the magazine, concentrating on the period of Ward's editorship, 1862–78. Appendixes discuss authorship of articles during this period and give brief biographies of principal contributors. There are no monograph studies of the other magazines indexed in the second volume of the *Wellesley Index—Bentley's Quarterly Review, London Review, New Quarterly Magazine, Nineteenth Century,* and *Scottish Review.*

It should be noted that, although not formally published, many of the doctoral dissertations on Victorian magazines are available for purchase in microfilm or photocopy, through University Microfilms. Such works are listed in *Dissertation Abstracts International.* Many of the published monographs listed above, such as those by Marchand, Mineka, Thrall, Everett, Nesbitt, and Bevington, are, of course, reprinted from or based on dissertations.

For some major magazines the best survey of their history and achievement has to be sought within their own pages. A classic example is A. R. D. Elliot's unsigned article "The *Edinburgh Review* (1802–1902)" (*Edinburgh Rev.,* 1902), an important contribution that traces the history of the magazine through its first century. As might be expected from one who was himself its editor, Elliot shows particular interest in the *Edinburgh's* succession of editors. The weakness of the article lies in its inadequate treatment of the later period of the magazine's history. The *Quarterly Review* similarly included a two-part article about itself in its centenary year, "The Centenary of the *Quarterly Review*" (*Quarterly Rev.,* 1909). The best account of the *Dublin Review* is an article by L. C. Casartelli, "Our Diamond Jubilee" (*Dublin Rev.,* 1896), which was reprinted in the magazine's centenary number as "The First Sixty Years" (*Dublin Rev.,* 1936). Many periodicals that exist for a considerable period of time do, of course, have an impulse to write about themselves, and such writings are often useful sources of information for the historian of periodicals. This topic is further examined in the sections that follow.

Magazines have also received serious attention in articles in scholarly periodicals. Among general studies, Geoffrey Carnall's "The *Monthly Magazine*" (*Rev. of English Studies,* 1954) surveys the magazine and its contents. In "German Influence upon Scientific Instruction in England 1867–1887" (*VS,* 1958) George Haines IV describes the founding of *Nature* in 1869 and discusses its aims.

Modern studies of magazines produced for specific interest groups or related to particular geographical areas can most profitably be sought in periodicals that have a special continuing interest in their subject. R. Barnes's historical study of "The *Midland Counties Illuminator*: A Leicester Chartist Journal" finds a natural place in *Transactions of the Leicestershire Archaeological and Historical Society* (1959). N. Campbell's "The *Edinburgh University Quarterly*, 1881–1882" is, logically, found in the *University of Edinburgh Journal* (1962). The *Proceedings of the Wesley Historical Society* (1969) is an obvious location for articles about Victorian Methodist periodicals, such as Frank Cumbers' "The *Methodist Magazine* 1778–1969."

The placement of an article in such a specialized scholarly periodical has the advantage for the author of insuring an interested readership. It is probably fair to say, too, that the more general scholarly periodicals have often been less than eager to encourage articles on the less obviously "major" magazines. For this reason, the appearance in *Victorian Studies* (1969) of a study by P. G. Scott of an aspect of evangelical publishing activity was particularly welcome. "*Zion's Trumpet*: Evangelical Enterprise and Rivalry, 1833–35" discusses the establishment and progress of the monthly magazine *Zion's Trumpet, Or the Penny Spiritual Magazine* and its rivalry with the *Gospel Herald, Or the Poor Christian's Magazine.*

Many scholarly articles, of course, have eschewed the general survey in favor of concentrating upon specific aspects of a magazine. A major concern has been with the identification of anonymous and pseudonymous contributors. F. W. Fetter's interest in nineteenth-century economic thought, evidenced in his "Economic Controversy in the British Reviews, 1802–1850" (*Economica*, 1965), prompted a number of articles on the identification of authors of economic articles in the *Edinburgh Review* (*Jour. of Political Economy*, 1953), the *Quarterly Review* (*Jour. of Political Economy*, 1958), *Blackwood's Edinburgh Magazine* (*Scottish Jour. of Political Economy*, 1960), and the *Westminster Review* (*Jour. of Political Economy*, 1962). Many writers have devoted themselves to the problems of identifying the authors of articles in specific magazines. B. M. Murray has examined "The Authorship of Some Unidentified or Disputed Articles in *Blackwood's Magazine*" (*Studies in Scottish Lit.*, 1967), with a further offering on the same subject in 1971–72. Edward M. White's

"Thackeray's Contributions to *Fraser's Magazine*" (*Studies in Bibliography*, 1966) offers a critical examination of previous attributions.

It might reasonably be expected that both *Victorian Studies* and *Victorian Periodicals Newsletter* would have printed important studies of specific Victorian magazines. In fact, *Victorian Studies* has shown surprisingly little interest in the detailed study of periodicals, though its pages have, of course, included many passing references to them. The issue for December 1969 was unique in being largely devoted to studies of the periodical press, with articles by Brian Harrison on the temperance press from 1830 to 1872, Stephen Coltham on "English Working-Class Newspapers in 1867," and Christopher Kent on "Higher Journalism and the Mid-Victorian Clerisy." The only article in the issue that was devoted to a specific journal, however, was Scott's discussion of *Zion's Trumpet*, already noted above.

If a survey of *Victorian Studies* proves rather disappointing to the student of periodicals, *Victorian Periodicals Newsletter* has much more to offer. Although always concerned explicitly with the Victorian periodical press, it is noteworthy that *Victorian Periodicals Newsletter* has changed its character from a very useful newsletter for the exchange of information to a more conventional, better produced, but in some ways less valuable magazine printing scholarly articles. In its earlier form *Victorian Periodicals Newsletter* offered an ideal forum for short specialized articles or extended notes on aspects of scholars' research. The first number, for example, in January 1968, included Rosemary T. VanArsdel's "Notes on *Westminster Review* Research," K. J. Fielding's "Re-Reading the *Examiner*," and Josef L. Altholz' "On the Use of 'Communicated' in the *Rambler*," all interesting short discussions based on larger research projects.

Surprisingly, although *Victorian Periodicals Newsletter* has produced several supplements and special issues devoted to specific topics, none of them has been concerned with an individual periodical. Important early contributions on individual magazines include John F. Byrne's two-part study of the *Reader* (1969) and H. B. de Groot's discussion of "Lord Brougham and the Founding of the *British and Foreign Review*" (1970).

With the transfer of *Victorian Periodicals Newsletter* from

Amherst to Toronto and the accompanying emphasis on full-length articles, the number of important extended discussions of individual magazines increased. The tone was set with two specialized studies in the first issue published in Toronto (Dec. 1973)—Cheryl Lively's "Truth in Writing: The Standard of Realism for the Novel in *Fraser's Magazine* 1830–1850" and Peter Allen and Cleve Want's "The Cambridge 'Apostles' as Student Journalists: A Key to Authorship in the *Metropolitan Quarterly Magazine.*" More recently, Robert H. Tener has discussed R. H. Hutton's connection with the *Inquirer* (1974), the *Prospective Review* and the *National Review* (1974), and the *Economist* and the *Spectator* (1975).

The new periodical *Publishing History*, launched by Chadwyck-Healey in 1977, under the editorship of Michael L. Turner, aims to include material on magazine and newspaper publishing.

Newspapers

Just as the most serious and scholarly studies of individual magazines have tended to concentrate upon a few well-known and influential titles, interest in newspapers has focused upon those major titles that survived into the twentieth century. There has been a strong tendency for such studies to appear in conjunction with an important anniversary in the paper's history, and frequently a sesquicentenary, a centenary, or some other anniversary has provided the impetus for some historical study.

By far the most important newspaper history is the four-volume *The History of the* Times (1935–47), which was written to commemorate the sesquicentenary of the *Times* in 1935. The scope of the work is precisely what its title professes: unlike some other newspaper histories, it is not attempting to give a history of events as seen through the columns of the *Times*. Because it was based on extensive research in the records of the proprietors of the paper, as well as in the national archives and in a large number of records in private and public ownership, the study is a substantial and scholarly one. The first three volumes covering the years 1785–1912 are particularly relevant to the historian of the Victorian period.

A similarly detailed and scholarly approach is adopted by David Ayerst in his important study Guardian: *Biography of a Newspaper* (1971), written to coincide with the 150th anniversary of the *Manchester Guardian*. Like *The History of the* Times, this is a carefully researched contribution to the history of British journalism that has drawn extensively on the records of the *Manchester Guardian*. The work largely supersedes an earlier work by William Haslam Mills, *The* Manchester Guardian: *A Century of History* (1921). As this work was tailored to meet the requirements of the centenary supplement of the *Manchester Guardian*, its style is much more popular and its treatment much more lightweight and cursory than Ayerst's.

Disappointing for its coverage of the Victorian period is a recent study by Harold Hobson, Phillip Knightley, and Leonard Russell, *The Pearl of Days: An Intimate Memoir of the* Sunday Times (1972). Of a total of 492 pages only sixty are relevant to the nineteenth century. The chapter by Harold Hobson entitled "The Obscure Years 1822–1915" leaves the reader with the impression that "the nineteenth century record is one of interest without significance" and the period covered, the "shabby and boring years" of the newspaper's history. Clearly, this is an area that would benefit from more detailed analysis.

Other newspapers celebrating 150th anniversaries in the twentieth century have been more reticent. Both the *Observer*, in 1966, and the *Morning Post*, in 1922, marked the anniversary with a special supplement, but no major monograph was commissioned to celebrate the occasion. It should not be forgotten that because of their longevity and influence some of the provincial papers may fall into the category of major newspapers. Few have prompted the appearance of as useful—although short—a study as *The Glorious Privilege: The History of the* Scotsman (1967), which was published to celebrate the sesquicentenary of this important provincial newspaper.

What is striking about the history of individual newspapers is the paucity of substantial and scholarly studies. Too often writers have resorted to lightweight treatment presented in a popular and journalistic style. Into this category fall such works as Robert J. Cruikshank's study of the *Daily News*, entitled *Roaring Century*

1846–1946 (1946), which is very much a history of the times as seen through the columns of the *Daily News.* A similarly gossipy style is adopted by John W. Robertson Scott in a series of studies of the *Pall Mall Gazette,* the two most notable titles of which are *The Story of the* Pall Mall Gazette, *of Its First Editor Frederick Greenwood and of Its Founder George Murray Smith* (1950) and *The Life and Death of a Newspaper: An Account of the Temperaments, Perturbations, and Achievements of John Morley, W. T. Stead and Other Editors of the* Pall Mall Gazette (1952).

Centenary studies have frequently fallen prey to this chatty or popular treatment, although in some cases there may be excellent reasons for it. For example, William Haslam Mills's study of the *Manchester Guardian,* noted above, reflects the requirements of writing for the centenary supplement of that paper. Other authors have been disadvantaged by the inadequacy of resources available to them. Certainly this is true of Lord Burnham, whose *Peterborough Court: The Story of the* Daily Telegraph (1955) had to be compiled from casual references in books, recollections of members of the staff, a few scrappy memoranda and letters, and from the files of the newspaper because official records had not been preserved. Under these circumstances, could we hope for more than "an impressionistic sketch of the *Daily Telegraph* and of some of the men who made it"?

Short studies of a variety of other newspapers have appeared. Examples include *The* Observer *1791–1921* (1922); J. B. Atlay's *The* Globe *Centenary: A Sketch of Its History* (1903); and, although the subject was not a "newspaper" in the accepted sense, Patricia M. Handover's *The History of the* London Gazette *1665–1965* (1966).

Although the twentieth century has seen its share of deaths of newspapers, remarkably few histories have been published to mourn such events. A notable exception was Wilfred Hindle's *The* Morning Post *1772–1937: Portrait of a Newspaper* (1937), The speed with which this study appeared after the demise of the *Morning Post* in September 1937 suggests that it is not the product of intensive research, and its style is decidedly popular. The occasion also prompted an article by W. Colgate entitled "Death at 164: The Portrait of a Newspaper" in *Queen's Quar-*

terly (1938). Another such work was G. Glenton and W. Pattison's *The Last Chronicle of Bouverie Street* (1963), written after the closure of the *News Chronicle (Daily News)* and the *Star*.

Newspapers are generally fairly meticulous in publishing special commemorative anniversary numbers, and these often contain useful historical articles. Although the *Observer* chose to celebrate its 175th anniversary (in a special supplement in 1966) much more usual are anniversaries marking 150, 100, and 50 years. The *Morning Post* (1922), the *Scotsman* (1967), and the *Guardian* (1971) all issued special numbers celebrating their sesquicentenaries. Much more common is the centenary, and this has been marked with a special issue by a variety of newspapers. Many weighty and influential newspapers like the *Sunday Times* (1921) have produced centenary issues, but so have some of the more popular papers too. Examples of these include the *News of the World* (1943), *Reynolds's Weekly Newspaper* (1950), and the *Weekly Dispatch* (1901). A centenary supplement may well prove to be the only source of information on a particular paper, as, for example, that of the *Morning Advertiser* (1894) and of the *Evening Standard* (1927), which makes a slightly tenuous claim to be a successor to the *Standard*.

Lesser anniversaries have also occasioned celebratory issues. Numerous newspapers have reached their fiftieth year, and the list of anniversary supplements is long and varied, including the *Daily Telegraph* (1905), the *Daily Mail* (1946), the *Star* (1938), and the *British Weekly* (1936). Less obvious anniversaries have also prompted special issues, as, for example, the diamond jubilee of *Lloyd's Illustrated Newspaper* (1902), or the thirtieth birthday of the *Echo* (1898), or even the ten thousandth number of the *Pall Mall Gazette* (1897).

Much valuable material on the history of individual newspapers can be found in editorial reminiscences, an area in which the history of Victorian journalism is particularly rich. *The Life and Adventures of George Augustus Sala, Written by Himself* (1895) is a good example. Such reminiscences, although inevitably subjective, may yield important information on specific newspapers, such as E. V. Lucas' account of his time on the staff of the *Globe*, in *Reading, Writing and Remembering* (1932).

Biographies of newspaper editors are numerous and often provide the most substantial account of a newspaper's history for a given period. Thus the most important study for the history of the *Morning Post* between 1853 and 1903 is still Reginald J. Lucas' *Lord Glenesk and the* Morning Post (1910). Inevitably, the great editors of the nineteenth century have attracted the most serious attention, and personalities such as J. T. Delane and C. P. Scott have each been the subject of several biographies. Notable among these are Arthur I. Dasent's *John Thadeus Delane, Editor of the* Times: *His Life and Correspondence* (1908) and John L. B. Hammond's *C. P. Scott of the* Manchester Guardian (1946). Similarly, students of less major newspapers will be very dependent upon works like John Saxon Mills's *Sir Edward Cook* (1921), which discusses his career on the *Pall Mall Gazette, Westminster Gazette,* and *Daily News.*

The last ten years have seen the increasing popularity of anthologies. Many of these contain only a brief historical introduction, like that by Asa Briggs in *The* Observer *of the Nineteenth Century,* compiled by Marion Miliband (1966). Rarer are longer introductory essays of the caliber of that in David Ayerst's *The* Guardian *Omnibus 1821–1971* (1973).

Despite the growing interest in the history of the British press in the nineteenth century many significant newspapers still lack any important study. The *Standard,* the *Westminster Gazette,* the *Daily Chronicle,* and the *Morning Chronicle,* for example, have all been neglected. Many others, such as the *Sunday Times* and the *Observer,* still await scholarly treatment of their history in the Victorian period.

Lesser Periodicals

As has been noted above, the more weighty studies of individual periodicals have tended to be devoted to the more obviously "major" or "significant" titles. In one of the most perceptive reviews of the *Wellesley Index* (*VPN,* 1973), P. G. Scott drew attention to the difference between "a study of the 'principal' periodicals (as exemplified in *Wellesley*), and a survey and analysis of all periodical debate (as discernible in the *Waterloo* listing)."

It is, of course, difficult—if not impossible—to uphold any absolute distinction between major and minor periodicals. Nevertheless, as several commentators have pointed out, it is clear that the attention of students of the nineteenth century has tended to concentrate upon a relatively small number of frequently studied titles rather than upon the whole diverse field of Victorian periodicals. For, beyond those "journals of relatively high calibre in the writing and editing, and of considerable reputation in educated circles" that Walter E. Houghton identifies as the object of *Wellesley*'s interest (*Wellesley Index*, Vol. II, 1972), there lie vast numbers of periodicals that are rarely consulted or studied. Michael Wolff's comment in "Charting the Golden Stream" (in *Editing Nineteenth-Century Texts*, ed. John M. Robson, 1967) still has applicability for the student of Victorian periodicals: ". . . what one must generally conclude about the current use of the periodicals is that scholars' needs have been met and that familiar evidence has been extracted only from familiar sources."

The progress of work on the *Waterloo Directory of Victorian Periodicals* and the resultant increase in our appreciation of the enormous number of periodicals that existed in the nineteenth century may well have provoked feelings of unease among students of the period. Nevertheless, there are still relatively few signs of any large-scale movement away from the preoccupation with a restricted range of principal titles. The vast majority of Victorian periodicals, therefore, still remain without any detailed studies, a situation that will continue throughout the foreseeable future. Thus the student must turn elsewhere for information; what other sources are available?

Sometimes, although there is no major study of an individual periodical, extensive information may be easily acquired from biographical or autobiographical works. The student seeking information about *Howitt's Journal*, for example, will find considerable material in C. R. Woodring's *Victorian Samplers: William and Mary Howitt* (1952). One of the best sources for information about the *Northern Tribune* is J. E. Courtney's *The Making of an Editor: W. L. Courtney 1850–1928* (1930). P. C. G. Isaac's study of *William Davison of Alnwick: Pharmacist and Printer* (1968) includes information about the *Alnwick Mercury*. Information about the *Illustrated Reporter* is given in an article on "The Trimbles of Enniskillen" in *Newspaper World* (1939).

For provincial newspapers especially, local histories may well prove a useful source of information. The problem is to identify the existence of such works. Often they are not recorded in bibliographies and can be traced only through the catalogues of local public libraries. Local histories, which derive much of their information from the area's press, frequently also devote attention to the press. H. H. Quilter's *Mid-Victorian Grantham* (1937) is described as "a commentary on the earliest numbers of the *Grantham Journal*." J. Burman's *Old Warwickshire Families and Houses* (1934) discusses issues of *Aris' Birmingham Gazette*.

Local public libraries may also contain unpublished studies of the local press, with information about specific periodicals. A manuscript "History of the Manchester Periodical Press" by F. Leary is in the Manchester Public Library. A manuscript study of the "Early Press of Middlesbrough" by J. Jennings is in the public library in Middlesbrough. The public library in Hull contains a typescript of extracts from a talk given by R. A. Brewer to the Cottingham Local History Society, entitled "A History of Hull Newspapers" (1967). The public library in York has scrapbooks compiled by T. P. Cooper on "York Newspapers, Printers, Booksellers, Authors, Artists, Etc." Many public libraries have built up their own collections of newspaper cuttings. The cuttings collection in the Sheffield Public Library, for example, includes an assortment of material relating to Sheffield newspapers in the nineteenth century.

Other periodicals in the area may prove useful sources of information, though it has to be admitted that lack of bibliographical guidance often makes it difficult to identify relevant items in such sources. The *Bedfordshire Times*, for example, has published short articles about the *Bedford Bee* (1944, 1960); *Bedford Mercury, Bedford Standard,* and *Beacon Gazette* (1948); *Bedford Budget* and *Pioneer* (1960); and *Bedford Standard* (1960). *Epworth Bells* was the subject of an article by R. Lawrence in *Lincolnshire Life* (1965).

There are, too, short articles on individual titles scattered more generally throughout the periodical literature. Again, deficiencies in bibliographical control may make these difficult to trace. It is particularly worth drawing attention to the extensive series of brief articles on provincial newspapers that was published in *Newspaper World* between 1938 and 1939 and to the longer but much less numerous articles that appeared in *Caxton Magazine* between 1901 and 1902, under the series title "Great Provincial Newspapers."

For many lesser titles, however, historical information can only be successfully sought within the periodical itself, most frequently in anniversary issues. As a new periodical's prospectus provided the opportunity to state the intended policy, so the anniversary issue offered editors an ideal occasion for reassessment—generally congratulatory—of past achievements and for stimulating interest for the future.

Anniversary issues, of course, vary widely in both length and depth of treatment. The characteristic centenary issues of provincial newspapers, for example, tend to specialize in short discursive articles. The *Blackburn Times* (1955) illustrates the point: it includes short articles, each of a single page or less, entitled "The *Times* Century of Progress," "The Local Newspaper and the Men Who Shaped It," and "In Succession as Editors." It also includes a longer piece: "The Story behind the Start of the *Blackburn Times*."

As with the centenary supplement of the *Wilts and Gloucestershire Standard* (1937), many centenary issues include a facsimile of the first number of the paper. They often also include statements of the principles that, it is claimed, have motivated the paper throughout its history. "Never an Unthinking Partisan," proclaims the heading of an article in the centenary supplement of the *Yorkshire Post* (1966).

However much one may lament their deficiencies, such anniversary numbers are the nearest we come to formal histories of many provincial newspapers. Of all anniversaries the centenary is the one most likely to produce a historical survey, though any other anniversary may bring a similar contribution. *Berrow's Worcester Journal* published a "250th Anniversary Number" in 1940, with an article on "The Story of *Berrow's*." The *Northampton Mercury* celebrated its 250th anniversary in 1970 with a supplement that contained a feature on "The Men Who Have Shaped the Destiny of the *Mercury*: Thirteen Editors in the Span of 250 Years." Such longevity is unusual, however, and more common anniversaries are those leading up to the century. In general, the most likely occasions are reasonably predictable, and such idiosyncracies as the celebration by the *Hereford Times* (1927) of "One Hundred All but Five" are—happily—rare. In addition to celebrating year anniversaries, newspapers may mark significant issue numbers (such as the 25,000th or the 50,000th) with historical articles.

In general, the anniversary number is a rather unsatisfactory and unsubstantial record from the historian's point of view. Sometimes, however, an anniversary prompts a more extensive and permanent record. The centenary of *Whitehaven News* was celebrated by the publication of a monograph by J. R. Williams, *The* Whitehaven News *Centenary: An Outline of 100 Years* (1952). The centenary of the *Birmingham Daily Post* was marked by a study by H. R. G. Whates, *The* Birmingham Post, *1857–1957: A Centenary Retrospect* (1957).

The anniversaries of magazines, when celebrated, may provide more solid information for the student. The fiftieth anniversary of *Mind* prompted a historical article, "Fifty Years of *Mind*," by W. R. Sorley (*Mind*, 1926). The first fifty volumes of the *Nineteenth Century* were discussed in an article by F. Harrison, "The *Nineteenth Century*, a Retrospect: The First Fifty Volumes 1877–1901" (*Nineteenth Century*, 1918). Although magazines usually celebrate their anniversaries in years, if at all, they may occasionally celebrate a particular number of issues. *Builder*, for example, celebrated its six thousandth issue with an article, "A *Builder* Milestone: The First 6,000 Issues" (1958).

Sometimes the anniversary is celebrated by another periodical. The 150th anniversary of the *Philosophical Magazine* was noted in an article in *Endeavour* (1949). The anniversary of the *Cork Examiner* was discussed in "A Cork Centenary" by J. J. Horgan (*Studies*, 1941). Other occasions for historical retrospect include final issues. The final issue of the *Portsmouth Times* (1928), for example, carried the paper's own historical survey, in an article headed "The *Portsmouth Times* 1850–1928."

Change of ownership could provide an occasion for historical recollections. When the *Peebleshire Advertiser* changed hands in 1931, it published a short history under the title "A Glance

Backwards and into the Future." So, too, an amalgamation or takeover might offer the opportunity for a backward glance, as when the *Cambridge Express* issued its final number before incorporation into the *Cambridge Weekly News* (1909). When, in 1968, the *Church Quarterly* succeeded the *Church Quarterly Review*, the new periodical included an article by R. C. D. Jasper on "The *Church Quarterly Review* 1875–1968."

VII

*The Identification of Authors: The Great Victorian Enigma**

Mary Ruth Hiller
The Wellesley Index

The Tradition of Anonymity

Shall I forever be concerned with the nameless?
John Milton, *Second Defense*, 1654

Through the centuries the tradition of anonymous authorship has provoked many echoes of Milton's cry, none more vociferous than those of modern Victorian scholars. No full-scale study has traced the historical development of journalistic anonymity that the Victorians inherited from earlier ages: studies like Archer Taylor and F. J. Mosher, *The Bibliographical History of Anonyma and Pseudonyma* (1951) and W. P. Courtney, *The Secrets of Our National Literature* (1908) have focused on the history of revealed authorship rather than the custom of anonymity itself; nor was it discussed by Walter Graham in his seminal work on *English Literary Periodicals* (1930). One might speculate that the tradition grew out of medieval forms of verbal entertainment and news dissemination typified by the nameless troubadours who traveled from court to court and sang the epics to which no author's name

* The author wishes to thank Walter E. Houghton for his helpful suggestions for this chapter, as well as for the many years of scholarly training she has received from him.

could be attached. Bookmaking during the Middle Ages was in the hands of the clergy, who maintained their control even after the printing press was invented. The assumption of literary anonymity was a natural outgrowth of the self-abnegating philosophy of the monastic system. Words spoke for themselves—authors were of no consequence.

When newspapers and periodicals began to appear in the seventeenth century, they were primarily propaganda organs for which hack writers produced what was ordered and, naturally, did not attach their names. Such writing was regarded with contempt by authors of repute. Early book reviews were mainly publishers' advertisements and often took the form of mere abstracts from the works being recommended. In the eighteenth century, anonymous or pseudonymous journalism continued, even in the more notable essay serials like the *Spectator* and the *Idler*. When the great age of the periodical dawned, with the commencement of the *Edinburgh Review* in 1802, the convention of anonymity was firmly entrenched. It was challenged briefly in 1809 when Richard Cumberland founded his *London Review* on the principle of signed articles. "A piece of crepe may be a convenient mask for a highwayman; but a man that goes upon an honest errand, does not want it and will disdain to wear it," proclaimed Cumberland in his "Introductory Address." But the *London Review* failed after four numbers, and the tradition of anonymous journalism continued unabated.

It has been estimated that between 1824 and 1900 close to seventy-five percent of the articles and stories published in monthlies and quarterlies were anonymous or pseudonymous; undoubtedly the figure would be much higher if weeklies were included. There were excellent reasons for the persistence of this tradition. One of the most persuasive was that writers could be more honest if they did not have to sign their names: an author could attack a friend without loss of goodwill, praise a "great" man without suspicion of toadyism, or criticize an institution that was a source of support without fear of reprisal. "We have anonymity to thank for many a critical article on the army and the navy, on foreign policy, or the London School Board, written from the inside," Walter Houghton pointed out in his introduction to the first volume of the *Wellesley Index to Victorian Periodicals*. And conversely, as John Morley, editor of the largely signed *Fortnightly Review*, commented in retrospect ("Memorials of a Man of Letters," *Fortnightly Rev.*, Apr. 1878), when writers had to sign their names, they often wrote what was expected from their position or character rather than what they honestly thought. Or else they did not write at all. Leslie Stephen went so far as to claim ("Anonymous Journalism," *St. Pauls Mag.*, May 1868) that persons in professions outside journalism would become unable or unwilling to contribute when signatures were required. He feared that periodicals would lose the best class of contributors and writing would devolve exclusively upon a professional class of journalists.

The question of honesty was a two-edged sword, and critics of the practice of anonymity were unanimous in their assertions that only with signatures would authors become responsible for their remarks and, therefore, honest as well as ethical. There was truth on both sides. But other advantages encouraged continuance of the traditional secretiveness. Individual articles or criticisms took on added prestige when associated with the larger corporate identity of well-known periodicals. This semioracular authority inclined the reader toward uncritical acceptance of what was written. Moreover, the mystery surrounding the unsigned article increased its appeal. If the author was unknown, he could as well be W. E. Gladstone as C. J. Bayley. Readers could speculate endlessly, and Victorian correspondence is full of just such speculations—a fact that now adds to the difficulties of those who seek out authorships!

There were further advantages to anonymity. Many young writers were able to get articles published that would never have appeared had the authors been required to put their unknown names to them. In addition, editors were able to exercise a useful flexibility. They could print several articles by the same author in a single issue if they so desired, and none would be the wiser. Also, they were freer to rewrite material to suit themselves, since the final product was not the author's responsibility. Thomas Hughes noted in "Anonymous Journalism" (*Macmillan's Mag.*, 1861) that anonymity benefitted three sets of persons: proprietors, whose property took on added value from the collective authority;

editors, who gained power and prestige as guardians of the mysteries; and writers, who could write anonymously with less thought and greater ease and who, by producing more copy, could make more money. Hughes added that the "consumer" was the only loser.

Occasional objections to anonymity were raised throughout the century. The debate that took shape has been described by Edwin Mallard Everett in *The Party of Humanity* (1939) and analyzed by Oscar Maurer in his "Anonymity vs. Signature in Victorian Reviewing" (*Univ. of Texas Studies in Eng.*, 1948). A useful bibliography of articles is given in the work mentioned above by Taylor and Mosher, *The Bibliographical History of Anonyma and Pseudonyma*, pages 178–79. As early as 1821 one enterprising publisher, Henry Colburn, broke the tradition of anonymous editorship and gave his *New Monthly Magazine* a boost up the ladder of success by publicizing the name of a well-known poet, Thomas Campbell, as editor. Occasionally signed articles and stories appeared in various journals, and after mid-century their frequency increased in some magazines, like *Fraser's* and the *New Monthly*. *Macmillan's* published signatures for approximately three fourths of its articles and stories from its beginning in 1859, but it was not until 1865, when the *Fortnightly Review* was founded on the stated principle of signed articles, that there was an explicit change in the tradition. Because of the recognized quality of its contributors, as well as of the essays themselves, the *Fortnightly* gained almost immediate influence, and the practice of anonymity declined further. By 1877 the economic value of the "star system" became apparent when James Knowles established the *Nineteenth Century* as the first completely signed periodical of the century (barring four pseudonyms), with the names of famous writers printed right on the cover. Nevertheless, the custom and rationale of anonymity held sway in many journals, like the *Athenaeum*, the *Edinburgh*, the *Quarterly*, and, for the most part, *Blackwood's*, until well into the twentieth century; ironically, the once signed *Fortnightly* published over five hundred articles without a real signature. Until June 1974, the prestigious *Times Literary Supplement* refused to name its critics—perhaps thereby achieving an influence greater than it otherwise would have had.

The Necessity of Identification

> So soon as I knew who Alpha was, his writing became
> modified to my understanding.
> F. W. Newman to A. H. Clough, 6 Dec. 1847

Because of the extensive practice of anonymity in Victorian periodical writing, modern scholars have been slow to make use of the special kinds of information available in these journals. Although some of the articles and stories were trivial, many were highly intelligent comments on all the burning interests of a rapidly changing society, in which politics, religion, law, and social customs were unstable and controversial. In this context, it may seem that only the articles themselves are important. What does it matter who the writers were? Do we truly need to know who is speaking when we read these essays? This last question must be answered with an emphatic affirmative because our understanding, as well as our utilization, of this material is irrevocably limited if we do not know its authors. Many of these articles are valuable precisely because of the writers, who were not only journalists but often the very persons involved with the issues—statesmen, clergymen, lawyers, bankers, teachers, doctors, artists, engineers, poets, inventors, novelists. To make full use of the potentially inexhaustible source of information that the periodicals offer, we must know who was saying what. An article on politics by Gladstone has a different importance from one by John Doe. The ambiguities of a discussion on a religious issue may be resolved by knowing that it was by the Catholic convert John Henry Newman, rather than by his liberal brother, Francis William Newman. The connotations of an article on Ireland are altered entirely if we discover that it is by an Irishman rather than by an English politician. A particular view of evolution may have unique implications when it is known to have been an early formulation by Herbert Spencer. Is a certain analysis of the novel by Thackeray? Or is it by Dickens, or Trollope, or Eliza Lynn Linton? If it is by Thackeray, it can be used to elucidate his concept of the form. But if we do not know who wrote it, it is merely "someone's" view of the novel, and much, if not all, of its value is lost.

Moreover, knowledge of the special context or importance of a particular article is not the only reason for learning the author's name. Because the periodicals were the testing ground for many concepts that later may or may not have evolved into book form, we need to know what articles each Victorian wrote if we hope to understand the author's thinking and development. For example, to follow Brougham's political thinking, we must be aware of his periodical writings. One expects to find John Arthur Roebuck writing vigorous political commentary, but a new dimension is added to his personality when one learns that he also wrote literary criticism. Disraeli's novels may be known, but are his short stories? Without knowing a Victorian's periodical writings, we cannot come close to a complete bibliography; because of the practice of anonymity, almost all published bibliographies have been deficient in this respect. Michael Collie's *George Meredith: A Bibliography* (1974), for example, lists, by admission, only Meredith's signed articles and makes no attempt to find his unsigned work. Where then can one look for possible answers to the question of what Meredith wrote anonymously or pseudonymously?

The Indexes

Not surprisingly, countless letters to the office of the *Wellesley Index* begin, "Could you please tell me the authors of the following articles?" For the first seven decades of the twentieth century, information concerning the authorship of anonymous and pseudonymous articles was scattered, intermittent, and difficult to obtain. Scholars were often forced to guess at authorships or to fall back on a collective identity, like "the *Edinburgh Review* stated . . ." or "the *Westminster Review* replied. . . ." The only comprehensive guide to the periodicals was *Poole's Index to Periodical Literature, 1802–1881*, with supplements to 1906 (rpt. 1938). *Poole's* is a subject index and remains the only such work available, but it suffers from serious defects. The subject headings are capricious, ill defined, and erratic. Taking as an example the subject of anonymous journalism, one encounters different entries under "Anonymous" and "Journalism, anonymous" and "Periodicals, anonymous." And how many items are totally missed? Nowhere will be found two *New Monthly Magazine* articles, "On Preserving the Anonymous in Periodicals" (1832) and "On the Anonymous in Periodicals" (1833), although *Poole's* claims to index the *New Monthly* (under the short title *Colburn's*). However, the limitations of *Poole's Index* as a subject index are minimal compared to its shortcomings as a guide to authorship. Authors' names are sometimes given in parentheses before articles, but the source of these attributions is not shown. The article may have been so signed (in which case the name may be a pseudonym or a title, like Marlborough, with no indication as to which Duke of Marlborough), or the indexer may have been guessing or using a marked file, that is, one in which the authors' names had been inserted in ink by someone else—correctly or incorrectly. Sometimes these entries are not the writers of the articles at all, but rather the authors of books being reviewed. Until recently there was no index to these "author" entries, so the harm they did was softened by the difficulties of retrieving them. But in 1971, C. E. Wall published a computerized *Cumulative Author Index for Poole's Index, 1802–1906*. No effort was made to investigate Poole's questionable identifications or to determine whether a name was a pseudonym. Therefore Wall's cumulation must be used with caution.

An author-subject index covering the years 1890–99, ambitiously called the *Nineteenth Century Readers' Guide to Periodical Literature* (ed. Helen G. Cushing and Adah V. Morris, 1944), attempted to improve on Poole's methods. Subject headings were standardized, and attempts were made to verify names and to distinguish between different men with the same title. Unfortunately the *Readers' Guide* includes only thirteen English periodicals, so its usefulness is circumscribed both by its time limits and by its meager coverage.

The principal source of information on the authorship of articles and stories in Victorian periodical literature is the *Wellesley Index to Victorian Periodicals, 1824–1900* (ed. Walter E. Houghton), published in four volumes (1966, 1972, 1978, and [projected] 1983). Approximately forty-five monthlies and quarterlies will be covered. A major research effort, extending over twenty-five years, will have gone into these identifications.

Each volume of the *Wellesley Index* consists of four sections. Part A includes, chronologically, every article in each periodical being covered, giving the title (with an explanation if the title is ambiguous), the pagination, and then the author (if known), followed by the evidence for that authorship. This emphasis on evidence is one of the principal innovations of the *Wellesley Index*. So far as possible the evidence is external: if not based on signature, then claimed by the author in a diary or a letter, or reprinted in a volume bearing his or her name, or attributed to the author by an editor or in a publisher's list, or otherwise assigned in relatively reliable sources like the *Dictionary of National Biography*, a bibliography, or a list of the author's writings attached to a biography. Sometimes, however, authorship is deduced only from an accumulation of clues, some of which are internal: subject, biographical remarks by the author, references to earlier identified articles that suggest a common authorship, or similarities in specific stylistic characteristics to identified works. The *Index* weights the evidence by marking "prob." or "?" if an authorship is not certain, but these are subjective designations. Readers see before them the reasons for any given attribution, albeit in brief form, and can judge for themselves its solidity. It should be noted that even when an article is signed the authorship may still be uncertain. Is "J. Chapman" John Chapman? And if so, which John Chapman? The *Index* identifies such signatures.

The first part of each chapter also contains a history of each periodical, with lists of editors, proprietors, and publishers, and a bibliography of studies pertaining to each journal. In addition, there is a "Note on Attributions" for each that describes what has been found in the way of publishers' lists, marked files, editors' correspondence, and so on. By reading these notes students see a broad spectrum of approaches to various problems of identification; each periodical is unique, and what has worked for one has not always worked for others.

The second section, Part B, lists every author, alphabetically, with brief biographical information and sources. Under each entry are placed all articles and/or stories in the journals indexed in that volume that are attributed to the author. Thus one finds a bibliography of periodical writings for each of the more than twelve thousand contributors in the *Wellesley Index*'s growing file of authors. Incidentally, the comprehensiveness of this roster makes the *Wellesley Index* a major biographical source for the Victorian period. Information from such scattered locations as obituaries in the *Minutes to the Proceedings of the Institute of Civil Engineers* or death certificates now at St. Catherine's House, London, are here coalesced.

To obtain a complete bibliography for some authors, one must check each of the four volumes, together with the Appendixes, because many Victorians wrote for periodicals that appear in different volumes of the *Index*. It is hoped that a cumulative author index will eventually be published, so that each author's full bibliography will appear in one place. However, in order to learn why any particular article has been attributed to a writer, it will always be necessary to consult the separate volumes.

The third section, Part C, lists all pseudonyms used in the indexed periodicals and gives the user's correct name, if identified. It may be generally known that "Major Goliah Gahagan" was W. M. Thackeray, but not that "Mr. Jolly Green" was Dudley Costello. Part C indexes these and hundreds of other pseudonyms.

The fourth section of the *Wellesley Index*, Volumes II, III, and IV, is the essential "Corrections and Additions" to the previously published volumes. Because scholarship is an open-ended process and new discoveries are continually being made, these Appendixes should not be ignored. For example, in the *North British Review*, between the years 1848 and 1850, there were twenty-two new attributions and four misattributions corrected in Volume II, all from a list found and analyzed after the publication of the main text of the *North British* in Volume I. Another example will be found in the "Corrections and Additions" in Volume III. It was only after the publication of Volumes I and II that a systematic search was made through the files of the Royal Literary Fund in London. These files, although not absolutely reliable (people forget, prevaricate, or become confused), have added many new identifications to the journals covered in the first two volumes of the *Index*.

In short, the *Wellesley Index* attempts to answer many specific questions: What articles were published, and when, in the periodicals being indexed? Who edited a specific issue? Who wrote a particular article? (The answer to this is not always forthcoming, because even the spy network of the *Index* has yet to ferret out all of the secrets from the hidden lives of the Victorians.) On what basis is a certain article assigned to Charles Kingsley? What were Walter Frewen Lord's dates, and where can more be read about him? Did George Meredith write any articles other than those he signed? Who called himself the "Old Forest Ranger"?

Aside from such questions, the uses to which the information in the *Wellesley Index* can be put are limited only by the imagination of future scholars. What were the principal issues in 1865? Which of Trollope's novels appeared originally as serials, and where? Were the writers for the major quarterlies drawn from the university, from business, or from politics, and what ratio of each? Who said what on the question of Reform in 1832? Were the Chartists vocal in the monthlies? What fraction of all contributors were women—perhaps hiding behind masculine or ambiguous names, like George Eliot and Currer Bell? Did the "Dissidence of Dissent" echo through the *Eclectic* and the *British Quarterly*? The questions go on and on. By consulting the *Index*, one can begin to formulate answers.

In addition to the *Wellesley Index*, a few other books have focused on the identification of authors. Hill and Helen Shine concentrated on attributions and evidence in their *The* Quarterly Review *under Gifford, 1809–1824* (1949), as did Alan Strout in *A Bibliography of Articles in* Blackwood's Magazine, *1817–1825* (1959). A recent study by Anne Lohrli on Dickens' *Household Words* (1973) has added greatly to our knowledge of the writers who contributed to Dickens' first weekly. An *Index to the London Magazine*, edited by Frank P. Riga and C. A. Prance, is about to be published. However, there are many important periodicals for which little or no such work has been done. Scattered attributions may be found in various articles, in single-author bibliographies, and in histories of some journals. But many authorships have yet to be uncovered. How then can one go about identifying the authors of anonymous or pseudonymous articles?

The Process of Identification: Where to Look for Clues

And article vi is by your Lordship's humble servant.
John Chapman to E. H. Stanley, 3 July 1861

In August 1975 research at the *Wellesley Index* on the author-ship of articles in the *Westminster Review* was drawing to a close. The *Westminster* was the principal radical quarterly of the nine-teenth century, but time for further research was running out. The attribution rate varied from editor to editor and proprietor to proprietor. During the early years of Jeremy Bentham's fund-ing, it was erratic; for the period of John Stuart Mill's editorship (1836–40), it was relatively complete, owing to the publication of Mill's *Letters* and to the "Mill-Fox copy," a marked file of part of the *Westminster* from which many attributions had been pub-lished in one edition of Caroline Fox's *Memoirs*. The twelve years of William Edward Hickson's editorship were well filled, thanks to the work of Rosemary VanArsdel and to the appearance of many initial signatures during that period. However, the era of John Chapman's long editorship (1852–94) remained hard to penetrate. For the first few years identifications were abundant because George Eliot was his assistant, and her *Letters* had an-swered many questions. Also, Chapman's three extant diaries, published in Gordon Haight's *George Eliot and John Chapman* (2nd ed., 1969), had offered many clues to fill in the blanks be-tween 1852 and 1860. But after that, information was hard to obtain. Chapman's letters were few and far between, perhaps be-cause his widow, who had edited the journal from his death in 1894 until its demise in 1914, first was robbed by an irresponsible niece, then went to the poorhouse. Having been rescued from that ordeal, she proceeded to give away Chapman's papers as memen-tos to casual visitors until she burned to death in her bed—under which boxes of his papers were stored.

For the researchers at the *Wellesley Index*, it was a classic ex-ample of the difficulties of attribution. No publishers' lists were extant, and the editor's papers, if not burned, were scattered and scarce. A Westminster Review Company had been formed in 1886, and the *Index*'s invaluable English researcher, Ann Palmer,

had probed the Public Record Office in England and had unearthed lists of stockholders in the company, some of whom had
turned out to be writers. But there were still many unidentified
articles. One final search was to be made.

On the theory that clues can often be missed the first time
through, a last look at Haight's *George Eliot and John Chapman*
was taken. This time a name, heretofore meaningless, rang a bell.
According to Haight, Edward Henry Stanley, fifteenth earl of
Derby, had been a financial backer of the *Westminster* in 1858.
But the name now took on new significance because it had been
learned that one of the stockholders in the Westminster Review
Company in 1887 was the same Lord Derby. Surely a man who
had invested his money in a journal from 1858 to 1887 must
have had some knowledge of its inner workings. And surely the
papers of the fifteenth earl of Derby, son of a prime minister and
himself a foreign secretary, were extant.

From the National Register of Archives (1975 update) it was
learned that a large collection of his papers was held by the Liverpool Record Office. A letter to Liverpool elicited the discouraging
reply that nothing was catalogued under *Westminster Review*.
However, it was suggested that the collection might have something under the names of individual correspondents. A list including John Chapman's name was sent, and the response was
instantaneous: there were approximately seventy-five letters from
Chapman to Stanley in the collection.

The suspense was hard to endure—would the letters yield anything in the way of attributions or would they discuss only the
finances of the Review? A microfilm was ordered, but meanwhile
Sheila Rosenberg, one of the *Index*'s advisory editors, who had
written a dissertation on Chapman and who lived in England, was
notified and hurried to Liverpool. Her letter to the *Index* began
with the classic "Stop the presses!"

It turned out that many of the letters contained lists of the
authors of articles in forthcoming issues of the *Westminster* or
enclosed tables of contents with the author's name written in be-
side each article. It was a dream come true, the kind of "find"
longed for by all who work on the identification of authorships.

This success story illustrates some of the methodology that has
been developed over the twenty years since the *Wellesley Index*

was conceived. To examine this methodology systematically, one must begin at the beginning, with a journal about which little or nothing is known.

In the first place, one examines the periodical itself, compiling a list of articles and noting the names of the publishers on the title page and any changes that occur. For the editors and proprietors, a good place to start is the *New Cambridge Bibliography of English Literature* (1969). In this edition, Henry and Sheila Rosenberg thoroughly updated the section on "Newspapers and Magazines," which gives not only known editors and proprietors, but also a selected bibliography of material on many individual periodicals. After the *New CBEL*, other specialized bibliographies are checked. *The Nineteenth-Century Periodical Press in Britain: A Bibliography of Modern Studies 1901 to 1971* (ed. Lionel Madden and Diana Dixon, supp. to *VPN*, 1975; rpt. 1976), lists articles, books, and dissertations on particular journals, newspapers, and individuals involved with periodicals. As the editors admit, "No bibliography of the nineteenth-century press could hope to be completely exhaustive." However, their work has gone a long way in aiding the search for relevant studies. To find what has been done since 1971, one turns to the "Checklists of Scholarship and Criticism in Victorian Periodicals" (ed. J. Don Vann et al.) published annually in the December issue of the *Victorian Periodicals Newsletter*. One caution must be observed with both the Madden-Dixon *Bibliography* and these checklists: sometimes no distinction is made between different periodicals with the same name. A study of the *National Review* (1855–64) may be indistinguishable from one on the *National Review* (1883–). The *London Review* (1829) can be confused with Mill's *London Review* (1835) and the *London Review* (1860–69).

After checking these references for twentieth-century studies, one considers the question of earlier works. The sources of information published before 1901 have not been tapped, except for those in the admittedly selective *New CBEL* bibliography. A so-called "big bibliography" covering the nineteenth century, similar to the one by Madden and Dixon for the twentieth, has been projected but has not yet been published. In the meantime, with the list of editors and proprietors, one turns to the *British Museum General Catalogue of Printed Books* (1931–65) and notes any memoirs, biographies, autobiographies, reminiscences, or the like. If one is lucky, there will be something to lead one further in the search. A memoir of an editor, for example, may well discuss contributors, print some correspondence, and list the editor's own articles.

Another helpful source to check is the journal itself. Periodicals often had anniversary issues in which the history was sketched, sometimes with lists of editors and contributors. The "Prologue to the Hundredth Volume" of the *New Monthly Magazine* (1854) is a case in point. Such essays may also appear whenever there is a change of editorship. In the *Eclectic Review* (1837), the departing editor, Josiah Conder, who had owned it since 1814, wrote a "Farewell Address," in which he obligingly printed a list of contributors. Then, in the very next issue of the *Eclectic*, an introductory essay by the new editor, an advertisement, as it might be called, announced anticipated contributors in order to entice readers. Some of these expectations may not have been realized, but the names constitute a record of possible writers. A similar source may take the form of an advertisement in a literary weekly, like the list of contributors to four volumes of the *Monthly Chronicle* found in an advertisement in the *Athenaeum*. (Other special issues are listed in Chapter vi of this volume.)

The research described above will yield a set of names—editors, proprietors, publishers, and possible contributors to the journal one is trying to "crack." The real detective work involves putting this material together with the articles published in the journal. This investigation is aided by the fact that, in spite of the tradition of anonymity, people were, by and large, proud of their creations and often bragged about them or at least left behind clues by which they could be identified.

The sleuthing may take many forms. The names should be pressed for more biographical details. If a person appears in the *Dictionary of National Biography* or in Boase's *Modern English Biography*, there will often be a list of sources from which the researcher summarized material. In the *DNB*, for example, under the lawyer Edwin Taylor is found "Field's Memoir of Taylor." Since the *DNB* article says that Taylor wrote for many periodicals, a search would be made for this "Memoir." It turns out to have been not a published book, as one might first surmise, but rather a very lengthy obituary published in the *Legal Observer*. This obituary provides many specific attributions that the writer of the *DNB* article omitted.

If a suspect held a post at a university or ever applied for one, a list of that person's anonymous writings may be found in the "Testimonials" written in the application for the post. Or if the author was ever short of money, the files of the Royal Literary Fund may reveal an application that cites anonymous articles. Or, if not specific articles, it may mention the particular periodicals and their dates—all foundations on which to build a case.

Every book by or about each suspect should be examined. There may be a bibliography, as in the case of John Stuart Mill. Such works vary in accuracy and are almost never complete, but, again, they may offer clues and, sometimes, firm attributions. The prefaces of all books by suspected authors are checked for such notations as "The last two chapters were previously published in the *Cornhill Magazine*" or "This work took shape from a series of articles written by the author twenty years ago." The first yields a quicker answer than the second, but the second may be the very evidence needed to clinch an attribution. If there is nothing helpful in the preface, a look at the chapter headings will often reveal notes saying where the material was first published. Or perhaps the book is a collection of essays, with no hint as to where they originally appeared. In this case, one may recognize the titles or subjects as ones that appear in the journal under examination. Lacking such recognition, one can turn to that poor, but indispensable, tool, *Poole's Index*, and hope to find the periodical— with volume and initial page—where the essay was first printed. Or if the book is dated after 1890, one may try the *Nineteenth-Century Readers' Guide, 1890–1899*. Examining, for example, a collection of short stories by Catherine Gore, *Mary Raymond and Other Tales* (1838), one finds that one of them is entitled "Napoleon at Fontainebleau." *Poole's Index*, happily, reveals that this title appeared in *Tait's Magazine*, "n.s. 1:659." One compares the story in *Tait's* with the reprinted version and finds that the two are substantially the same. And, if one were investigating Catherine Gore as a known contributor to the *New Monthly*, in which she had signed some stories, one would now know that she should also be placed on the list of contributors to *Tait's Magazine*.

It is possible that a book by one of the suspects will give every appearance of being an original work, not a collection of re-printed essays or a series of chapters made up of articles. But one should not give up too soon. As Joanne Shattock pointed out in "Spreading It Thinly" (*VPN*, 1976), writers of periodical articles often got as much mileage out of an article as possible, and some of them used material again and again, rewritten, rehashed, re-formed, but essentially the same. An excellent example of this technique is the work of J. H. Rigg, an editor of the *London Quarterly Review*. Rigg published many books during his life-time, many of which did not claim to contain reprints of his articles in the *London Quarterly*. But a close comparison of these books with many anonymous articles in the journal yields numer-ous verbatim passages, in material separated by as much as forty years. For Rigg, clearly, if a point was worth making once, it was worth making again, and why use new words every time? So the anonymity of Rigg's periodical writing begins to be solved, and the development of his ideas is revealed in a manner heretofore unknown. Of course, the chance of plagiarism must be kept in mind, but as a pattern evolves, plagiarism can usually be spotted. A writer may steal another's words now and then and not be caught, but not consistently over a number of years.

In addition to printed matter, a continuous search should be made for marked files of the periodical. Markings vary greatly in reliability and in extent, but there are many "lost" sets that were annotated by editors, subeditors, publishers, or authors that may now reside in the most unlikely places. One never knows when a valuable find is just around another corner—or across another ocean. An inexhaustible quest for marked files of the *Westminster Review* was described by Rosemary VanArsdel, in "Notes on *Westminster Review* Research" (*VPN*, 1968). She discussed some of the inscribed copies known to have existed and the hunt for them that had been made in forty libraries in the United King-dom and in two hundred fifty in the United States. Almost three hundred queries, and still a find was missed! It was not until 1976 that a marked file was exhumed at the Fisher Library of the University of Sydney, Australia. This file covered Mill's *London Review*, the *London and Westminster*, and the *Westminster* under Hickson, up to May 1843. Whose copy it was has not been determined. The markings, though not complete, are remarkably accurate, and the copy was said to have come to the Fisher Library from the Parliamentary Library of New South Wales. Like the Edward Henry Stanley–John Chapman letters at Liverpool, the marked Fisher set was a buried treasure, unearthed after all possibilities had presumably been exhausted.

Many periodical series have been broken up over the years, so that in a current collection only a few issues may be marked. A set may originally have belonged to someone who knew only a few of the writers, and hence the markings may be sporadic. Or an owner may have merely guessed at authorships and written in those suspicions; therefore the markings may be totally unreliable. But in spite of the uncertainties surrounding them, marked copies are valuable aids in the quest for authorships. Librarians should become aware of the search for such copies so that they can familiarize themselves with those under their care and inform scholars of their existence.

Printed material and marked files are not enough, however. One must use manuscript sources. Publishers' records, like Blackwood's Contributors' Book or the Longman's list of contributors to the *Edinburgh Review*, 1847–1900, are invaluable. A good sampling of the possibilities will be found by reading the "Notes on Attributions" for each of the periodicals included in the *Wellesley Index*. And the search goes on. A new British project is attempting to bring some order out of the chaos of publishers' records. The firm of Chadwyck-Healey (Bishops Stortford, Hertfordshire) is in the process of microfilming publishers' records and making guides to these films. To date, the following indexes have been published: *Index of Authors and Titles of the Publishers Kegan Paul, Trench, Trübner, and Henry S. King, 1853–1912; Index to Correspondents with the Publishers George Allen and Co., 1893–1915;* and *Index and Guide to the Lists of Publications of Richard Bentley and Son, 1829–1898,* edited by Michael L. Turner. The expensive microfilm of the actual accounts may be purchased from the publisher or borrowed from a library that subscribes to the Center for Research Libraries in Chicago.

Apart from such records, the letters, diaries, and accounts of the editors, proprietors, and contributors often yield highly reliable information concerning the authorship of articles. But where are they? Since many British collections have made their way to America, the *National Union Catalog of Manuscript Collections* is a source to be checked, as is Philip Hamer's *Guide to Archives and Manuscripts in the United States* (1961). The location of manuscripts in the United Kingdom is harder to ascertain. The Historical Records Commission and the National Register of Archives are continually enlarging their files and should be queried. *Select Biographical Sources* (ed. Philip Hepworth, 1971) lists the locations in England of manuscripts by approximately fourteen hundred British authors. Hepworth also describes other publications, such as his own *Archives and Manuscripts in Libraries* (2nd ed., 1964), and discusses in detail how to use the files of the National Register of Archives, with its three catalogues (person, subject, and topographical). Other possible guides to manuscript locations are the *Edinburgh University Library Index to Manuscripts* (1964), H. O. Coxe, *Catalogue of Manuscripts in the Oxford Colleges* (1852; rpt. 1972), and Paul Morgan, *Oxford Libraries outside the Bodleian* (1973). One of the many projects initiated by the Research Society for Victorian Periodicals was the formulation of a checklist of manuscript materials relating to Victorian periodicals. This project was described and a first list published by the late H. W. McCready, in "Towards a Checklist of Manuscript Resources for Victorian Periodicals" (*VPN*, 1974). Major manuscript collections discovered by the *Wellesley Index*, like publishers' records, are described in its "Notes on Attributions" for each periodical.

Another possibility suggests itself if one knows where an editor, proprietor, or contributor lived, went to school, or died. The librarians of local repositories are glad to see whether they hold manuscript materials relating to the writer in question. A will preserved at the Registry of Wills (Somerset House, London) can supply a lead to descendants who may have papers stored in their attics or back rooms. For diaries and autobiographies, William Matthews' *British Diaries: An Annotated Bibliography of British*

Diaries Written between 1442 and 1942 (1950) and his *British Autobiographies: An Annotated Bibliography of British Autobiographies Published before or Written before 1951* (1955) may be checked. Also, a newer publication, John S. Batts's *British Manuscript Diaries of the Nineteenth Century: An Annotated Listing* (1976), should be consulted.

Having made as much effort as time, resources, and imagination will allow, through the use of printed books, marked files, and manuscript materials, what can one do about the mysteries that remain? Much of the material described yields hints and clues, but no firm attributions. It is absolutely essential—and this cannot be stressed too much—that the articles themselves be read. Unless the evidence of authorship is firm beyond a doubt, there is no substitute for seeing that every article being attributed to a writer fits his or her particular crotchets—subject, biographical facts, style, and any other evidence in hand. The articles themselves often contain clues to their authorship. For example, in an article in the *Westminster Review* entitled "The Suppressed Sex" (1868), the anonymous author tells us that he went to reside near Antioch College twelve years before and that he is familiar with Harvard and with the University of Virginia. There is one man on the list of known contributors to the *Westminster* who fits these particular biographical facts: Moncure Conway. No other writer conforms to these precise details, so with this evidence his authorship is virtually certain.

Besides biographical facts, the articles may reveal distinctive stylistic peculiarities that will help to solve the mystery. The fact that one known reviewer on economics constantly uses italics and another never does may help distinguish between their reviews. Or if articles by a familiar author always contain a large number of footnotes and a review thought to be that writer's has none, then the identification is suspect and must be tested further, or perhaps abandoned. In the process of trying to attribute articles it must be kept in mind that disproving a hypothesis is often valuable protection against the worst of sins, misattribution, so negative results should not lead to discouragement. One is always on the lookout for distinguishing characteristics that separate a given author from the general run of periodical writers. Mary Margaret Busk, for example, often ends her reviews with the phrase "We lay down our pen. . . ." Since she also uses extensive extracts, she becomes a strong suspect when these two characteristics are found in a journal for which she is known to have written. Similar hallmarks—the term *con amore*, extravagant coined language ("shopocracy")—point to W. H. Leeds, in reviews on architecture. A comparison of style in two articles on the same subject may confirm or disprove a hypothesis of common authorship, although it is almost never sufficient in itself for an identification.

If an article or story is signed with initials or a pseudonym, an immediate clue is available. The Victorians often used one or the other to mask their identities or to fulfill the letter of the law of anonymity, while letting their friends know who wrote the paper. Sometimes initials are the true initials of the writer; therefore, all such signatures should be checked against the list of known contributors. If any fit, a suspect is in hand, but further evidence must be sought to support the attribution. One cannot rely on initials alone. For example, William Edward Hickson signed some of his articles with his full initials, W. E. H., but one article so signed during the period in which he was contributing was a highly professional discussion of architecture. Although Hickson was a broadly knowledgeable man, he was not an architect. It turned out that the initials were a printer's error and should have read W. R. H., since the author was William R. Hamilton, an architect. (See *Foreign Quart. Rev.*, 1836, p. 161, and compare Hamilton's *Letters to the Earl of Elgin on the New Houses of Parliament*, 1836.) Moreover, at a different time and in a different journal, the initials W. E. H. indicated not Hickson but William E. Hodgson. All pseudonyms can be checked in Halkett and Laing, *Dictionary of Anonymous and Pseudonymous English Literature* (1926–32, 1962), for possible solutions and in the American equivalent, William Cushing, *Initials and Pseudonyms: A Dictionary of Literary Disguises* (1885, 1888). But it must be remembered that the former covers only books and pamphlets, and the latter rarely mentions articles. Part C of the *Wellesley Index* is at present the only list of pseudonyms and initials in periodicals.

If none of these sources yields a likely possibility and the pseudonym is a three-initial signature, there is another approach.

The authors in the appropriate period of the chronologically arranged *English Catalogue of Books* can be checked for possible solutions. An article on the law courts in *Fraser's Magazine* in 1861, for example, was signed T. E. H. Last names beginning with H were skimmed in the appropriate volume of the *English Catalogue*, in a search for an author with the first initials T.E. writing on law. Thomas E. Holland appeared as a potential author, and further research supported the identification. If an article is on the army or on one of the universities, the *Army List* for that year or the university alumni lists can be examined for men with the appropriate initials. A name gleaned in this way will only be a possibility, not a firm attribution, but further work, it is to be hoped, will prove or disprove the theory.

Is it ever possible simply to read an unsigned article and find enough clues for a hypothesis? Yes, it happens, but not often. A case in point was a review of Aristophanes in the *Eclectic Review*, 1824. The article was a very learned analysis, so a classics scholar was immediately suspected, but none was on the list of contributors to the *Eclectic*. Therefore, the classicists in the *New Cambridge Bibliography of English Literature* were considered, as were those in John Edwin Sandys' *History of Classical Scholarship* (1908–21). Since the *Eclectic Review* was primarily a Dissenters' journal, the search was for an author who was neither Anglican nor Catholic. The name of Thomas Mitchell came forward because Mitchell had refused to sign the Thirty-Nine Articles. Moreover, he had translated Aristophanes. Further research showed that he had reviewed Aristophanes in the early *Quarterly Review* indexed by Hill and Helen Shine, as mentioned above. A close comparison of his earlier review with the one in the *Eclectic* revealed an unusual number of parallels in ideas, phraseology, and point of view, which supported the attribution. Then it was noted that Mitchell had also written on Schlegel in the *Quarterly*, and that the *Eclectic* reviewer frequently quoted Schlegel. At this point the attribution to Mitchell was made, not with certainty, but with the weight of the evidence pointing strongly to its accuracy. A search for Mitchell's manuscripts might yield definite proof, but the loss of papers may preclude such an opportunity. In any event, Mitchell is now added to the list of contributors to the *Eclectic* and further research may uncover more of his work.

Pitfalls

How you could take it for his I cannot conceive.
George Eliot to Sara Sophia Hennell
[10 Jan. 1853]

There is no single source of information on the authorship of anonymous and pseudonymous articles that has proven to be infallible. The best of publishers' lists has errors. Even a signed article can be misleading—the signature of John Chester may, in fact, be that of John Graham, Bishop of Chester. Some of the problems have been touched on above: the often erroneous speculations found in correspondence, the inaccuracy of some bibliographies, the possibility of plagiarism, and the dangers of reliance on initials that may or may not be correct or that may be odd combinations, like P.M.Y. for Margaret Mylne. An article on "Darwinism and Religion" (*Macmillan's Mag.*, 1871) signed A.B., illustrates the pitfalls of initial signatures. The article was attributed by the *Wellesley Index* to Alexander Bain on the basis of the signature, which was known to have been used by him in that magazine, and of the subject, which was of interest to him. Many accurate identifications have been based on just such a combination. A close comparison of the article with others known to be by Bain might have prevented the error, but the importance of such comparisons had not yet been learned. And such a comparison, though it might have ruled out Bain, could not have revealed the true author, who is now known to have been Arabella Buckley, a discovery made after a letter from A. R. Wallace to Darwin mentioning Miss Buckley's review in *Macmillan's* was noted in James Marchant, *Alfred Russel Wallace: Letters and Reminiscences* (1916).

Eileen Curran has discussed some of the particular hazards involved in identifying articles written by foreigners, often refugees in England, in "Reviews of Foreign Literature: Some Special Problems" (*VPN*, 1973). Did they change or anglicize their names? Who were their translators, and did the translators write portions of the articles or merely translate? Was there more than the usual amount of editorial tampering with foreigners' material?

The question of editorial meddling is a difficult one for many periodicals. Although the extent of such alterations varied from one editor to another, by and large, they felt responsible for the material they printed and therefore considered themselves free to alter articles as they saw fit. One Victorian went so far as to say that "we are bound to disbelieve all reports of articles in Reviews being written by single individuals"! When Philip Henry Stanhope, Lord Mahon, reprinted some of his *Historical Essays* (1849), he remarked acidly that one of them was "the groundwork of the 8th Article of the 97th Number of the *Quarterly Review*. But having there been incorporated with observations, in several of which the writer does not concur, he thinks proper to print his own as he originally wrote them." A collection of editorial correspondence illustrating editor-author responses to this problem would be a fascinating study.

In his introduction to Volume II of the *Wellesley Index*, Walter E. Houghton analyzed the principal causes of errors found up to that time in the *Index*. Two patterns emerged: the assumption that a credible name (like Constance Eaglestone) was not a pseudonym, when in fact it was, and the tendency to falsify a correct surname by giving it someone else's first or middle name and life dates (James Purves was not James Liddell Purves, as was first assumed). Because of the awareness of these two primary problems, the misattributions from such mistakes decreased enormously in succeeding volumes of the *Index*, although it is still sometimes difficult to determine whether a credible name is or is not a pseudonym.

Misattributions can also be made inadvertently by following leads to erroneous conclusions. This can be avoided only with extreme care and sometimes only with good luck. For example, in the *Foreign Quarterly Review* (Apr. 1842), an article entitled "The French Police" was attributed to George Stovin Venables on the basis of a letter from the soon-to-be editor, John Forster, dated 15 March 1842, saying that Venables and Thackeray would have articles in "this number," meaning the April issue. Since Venables was known to write on French subjects, the article was a likely choice, and the evidence looked conclusive. However, there is many a slip between an editor's plans and publication. Apparently the Venables article was delayed until July, for when Venables' own "Journal" was found in the National Library of Wales, it was seen that he referred frequently to his article on Fouqué that appeared in July, but did not once mention "The French Police" in April.

The question of collaboration makes some identifications particularly tricky. Michael and John Banim collaborated on a book called *The O'Hara Tales* (1825). An article in *Tait's Magazine* was signed "Author of the O'Hara Tales." Was it by John, by Michael, or by both, like the book? Luckily, in this case Michael attributed the story to his brother John in the preface to *A Bit O' Writin'* (1838), where it was reprinted. Another kind of problem is illustrated by the collaboration between T. P. Thompson and Jeremy Bentham in an article entitled "The 'Greatest Happiness' Principle" (*Westminster Rev.*, July 1829). This article was an answer to a serious attack by Macaulay that had been published in the *Edinburgh Review* (Mar. 1829). Thompson reprinted the *Westminster* essay in his *Exercises* with no mention of a collaboration, but Bentham had claimed in the *Examiner* (5 July 1829) to have furnished Thompson with "a few pages composed of memorandums, forming a sort of history of the Greatest Happiness Principle." George L. Nesbitt, in his *Benthamite Reviewing: The First Twelve Years of the* Westminster Review, *1824–1836* (1934), sketched the whole story in broad strokes, concluding that the first four pages of the article were by Thompson, written as an answer to the *Edinburgh,* and that the remaining ten were a condensation of Bentham's material. However, a closer comparison of Bentham's manuscript (dated 2–9 June 1829) in the Bentham Papers at University College, London, entitled "Article on Utilitarianism" with the article published in the *Westminster* showed that only passages on pages 258–60 and 267–68 were condensations of Bentham's material and that the remainder of the article was by Thompson alone.

Misattributions may be made through carelessness, hasty generalizations, mistaken authorities, or misinterpretations. To avoid them, all evidence must be scrupulously sifted and the possibilities for error constantly kept in mind. But if scholars proceed with due caution and realize that they are often dealing with probabilities rather than certainties, the accuracy of identifications is bound to increase.

Future Directions

> Few things are impossible to diligence and skill.
> Samuel Johnson, "On the Art of Flying,"
> *Rasselas*, 1759

Writing in the *Fortnightly Review* in 1877, Mark Pattison, rector of Lincoln, proclaimed that the monthly periodical seemed destined to supersede books altogether. He concluded that the periodicals "cannot be disposed of by slightly looking into them; they form at this moment the most characteristic and pithy part of our literary produce." In order for the modern scholar to mine this rich and complex source, he must have the tools with which to dig. An accurate and complete subject index, correcting the omissions and mistakes in Poole's early endeavor, is urgently needed. A book-review index has often been called for. Author indexes are essential for divers monthlies and quarterlies that are not in the *Wellesley Index*, as well as for many important weeklies. For example, the marked files of the *Athenaeum* in the offices of the *New Statesman*, if edited and published, would add significantly to the bibliographies of many vital Victorian figures, as Jeanne Fahnestock has shown in her "Authors of Book Reviews in the *Athenaeum*, 1830–1900: A Preview and a Sample" (*VPN*, 1972). A similar statement can be made for *Punch*'s contributors' ledgers at Punch Publications Ltd. (see John Bush Jones, "An Author-Title Index to *Punch*, 1841–1901," *VPN*, 1974) and for many others. The more specialized journals, like those on the theater, art, economics, philosophy, science, and psychology, would become much more valuable and useful if author indexes were compiled for them. Those listed in the *New Cambridge Bibliography of English Literature* are a good place to begin.

If the periodical writers of the nineteenth century are not to suffer the ignominious fate to which Lord Byron consigned them in his "English Bards and Scotch Reviewers,"

> Condemned at length to be forgotten quite
> With all the pages which 'twas thine to write,

there is much to be done. The *Wellesley Index* is a beginning. Though in the end it may have to be admitted that in some cases all evidence for an authorship has been lost or destroyed, those who venture on the quest should take courage from John Morley's optimistic remark one hundred years ago, "It is impossible for a writer of real distinction to remain anonymous."

VIII

Circulation and the Stamp Tax

Joel H. Wiener
City University of New York

Newspapers, commented one nineteenth-century wit, "resemble fashionable ladies of the West End in that they are more concerned with their *figures* than with their *morals*." It was an observation more appropriate perhaps to the 1930s than to the comparatively sedate middle decades of the nineteenth century. But the benchmarks of journalistic expansion during the Victorian period appear at every turning of the historical road: increased literacy, technological innovation (compositors' rooms alone remained relatively immune to the spread of machinery until late in the century), a dramatic decline in the price of paper, more efficient distribution of copy, the removal of financial restraints, even an expanded servant class to cater to the literary needs of its social superiors. The railway, the telegraph, and the avid consumer of penny tracts became triune symbols of the new age of popular journalism. If it remained for Alfred and Harold Harmsworth to complete the conversion of the press from an engine of ideas into a "branch of commerce" (the words are those of Kennedy Jones, a key lieutenant in the Harmsworth empire), the groundwork was nonetheless laid by the Victorians.

Newspapers experienced more spectacular circulation breakthroughs than magazines, beginning in the 1840s when, for the first time, illustrated weeklies gained readerships that reached into the hundreds of thousands. With the repeal of the newspaper stamp duty in 1855, expansion of the press moved one step further. Penny dailies—the *Daily Telegraph* (1855), the *Morning Star* (1856), and the *Standard* (1858) are the best known—came into existence, to be followed a decade later by W. T. Stead's *Northern Echo* (first published at Darlington in 1870) and other half-penny journals. In 1896 the readership equivalent of the journalistic sound barrier was broken when *Lloyd's Weekly Newspaper* became the first British journal to cross the one million mark. And within a few short years, the *Daily Mail*, the supreme exemplar of the "new journalism," brought Victorian journalism to a peak by achieving the legendary goal of more than one million daily readers.

Victorian journalism and its steady growth have been assiduously studied in recent years, and the products of this new academic industry are almost as numerous, if not as cheap, as their subjects. The impressive bibliography compiled by Lionel Madden and Diana Dixon, entitled *The Nineteenth-Century Periodical Press in Britain: A Bibliography of Modern Studies, 1901–1971* (supp. to *VPN*, 1975; rpt. 1976) illustrates the range of research being done on Victorian journals, as does the excellent revision of the section on "Newspapers and Magazines" by Henry M. and Sheila K. Rosenberg (*New Cambridge Bibliography of English Literature*, III, ed. George Watson, 1969). Additional testimony (if it is needed) to the central place of journalism in the printed culture of the nineteenth century is provided by the success of the Research Society for Victorian Periodicals and of its progeny, the *Victorian Periodicals Newsletter*.

With considerable effectiveness, scholars are exploring journalistic sources to illuminate the cultural and political byways of a society in the throes of change. They are producing studies of publishing companies, biographies of prominent journalists, and economic and cultural analyses of the influence of print, not to mention conventional treatises on the relationship between political events and journalistically inspired opinions. In one important respect, however, much of the recent academic work remains seriously deficient: this is in the charting of specific circulation figures for journals. For if the ups and downs of some newspapers' circulations are well known (though rarely in adequate detail), what of the monthly, quarterly, and weekly magazines—and daily and weekly newspapers—whose triumphs and failures were not sufficiently noteworthy to be included in general histories of the period, but whose circulation figures might give a sense of the influence of journalism? Is it possible to delineate these figures with any accuracy? And if the possibility exists, where is the student to turn in search of such information?

Secondary Sources: General Studies

It must be stated at the outset that nineteenth-century circulations are elusive figures. They are frequently immune to the probings of even the most diligent researcher and are much more easily rendered in the abstract than in the concrete. The Victorians were blissfully ignorant of the virtues of "net sales certificates" (although accountants began to certify some publishers' claims beginning in the 1870s), and they had no interest in establishing an equivalent to the Audit Bureau of Circulations in order to validate claims. Instead they relied on the integrity of publishers' pronouncements to whet readers' and advertisers' curiosity about circulation. And such pronouncements—with the notable exception of the parliamentary returns on the newspaper stamp duty—provide the basis for most of the secondary literature about circulation.

To search for information about circulation in the secondary sources is bound to be a frustrating experience, but two brief studies are exceptions of considerable importance. They are Alvar Ellegård, "The Readership of the Periodical Press in Mid-Victorian Britain" (*Göteborgs Univ. Årsskrift*, 1957; Part II is usefully rpt. in *VPN*, 1971), and A. P. Wadsworth, "Newspaper Circulations, 1800–1954," a paper read at the Manchester Statistical Society (Manchester, 1965). Ellegård primarily analyzes periodicals of the 1860s, while Wadsworth confines his discussion of circulation to newspapers, which are, at best, a selective and partial form of journalism. Yet both authors raise issues of methodology and substance that are likely to prove valuable to the student in search of statistical material. Ellegård, in particular, deals critically with the problems involved in making use of the stamp returns. Less helpful conceptually but interesting, nonetheless, is Richard Altick's *The English Common Reader: A Social History of the Mass Reading Public, 1800–1900* (1957), especially Appendix C, "Periodical and Newspaper Circulation." Altick prints sample estimates of the circulations of many Victorian journals and, usefully, reveals to his readers the divers sources upon which he bases his conclusions. A close reading of Altick yields insights into the complexity and randomness of the problem of calculating Victorian readerships.

Beyond Ellegård, Wadsworth, and Altick there are only a few general works to which the student can turn for information about circulation. All three writers (and most others who have dealt with circulation statistics) rely heavily upon James Grant's monumental three-volume *The Newspaper Press, Its Origin, Progress, and Present Position* (1871–72) for enlightenment. Grant's narrative suffers, predictably, from the limitations of age: it does not, for example, delineate the more striking aspects of the growth of popular journalism in Victorian Britain, since these events occurred primarily after the book was written. But Grant's inside knowledge of journalism was unrivalled (he was editor of the *Morning Advertiser* for more than twenty years), and his numerous estimates of circulation—for periodicals as well as for newspapers—must be regarded, in most instances, as definitive. At a minimum, they provide an invaluable basis with which to test the validity of circulation figures derived from other sources. H. R. Fox Bourne's *English Newspapers: Chapters in the History of Journalism* (2 vols., 1887) is a work similar in conception to Grant's, though not as penetrating. It is, as its title suggests, an analysis of the history of newspapers, and although Bourne's hypotheses about individual circulations are well based, they are not founded on the wealth of personal information available to Grant. Much more recent is Arthur Aspinall's masterful *Politics and the Press, c. 1780–1850* (1949). Aspinall is concerned with the readership of journals rather than with their actual circulations (the two aspects interlock), but there is much to be learned from a careful reading of the book, especially since Aspinall's observations about readership are drawn from innumerable private archives and letters.

Many other studies of Victorian journalism shed light on

aspects of circulation and may be of either general or limited interest to the student, depending upon the focus of research. There is, for example, an expanding body of secondary literature on the history of popular culture, a subject integral to an understanding of Victorian journalism and, by its very nature, concerned with the expansion of consumer demand. The following books (by no means inclusive) all contain useful information about the circulation of popular journals: R. K. Webb, *The British Working-Class Reader, 1790–1848* (1955), which is concerned primarily with the spread of literacy; Raymond Williams, *The Long Revolution* (1961), a broad analysis of the redefinition of working-class culture; Louis James, *Fiction for the Working Man, 1830–1850* (1963), a pioneering study of the distribution of popular fiction in the 1840s; and Joel H. Wiener, *The War of the Unstamped* (1969), and Patricia Hollis, *The Pauper Press* (1970), both of which deal with the opposition to statutory restraints on the press. In the related area of critical bibliographical analysis, Joel H. Wiener's *A Descriptive Finding List of Unstamped British Periodicals, 1830–1836* (1970) and *The Warwick Guide to British Labour Periodicals, 1790–1970: A Check List* (ed. Royden Harrison, Gillian Woolven, and Robert Duncan, 1977) contain detailed information about the circulation of popular journals.

Secondary Sources: Studies of Individual Periodicals

Studies of particular journals frequently incorporate information about circulation. But most Victorian journals have not yet found their historian, and only a small number have been systematically combed for readership figures. What exists in this area can be best described as a lightweight portmanteau containing a few definitive exegeses about circulation, a great many guesses and tentative conclusions, or, in some cases, nothing at all. Some newspapers have been satisfactorily penetrated from the circulation standpoint, notably in *The History of the* Times (4 vols. in 5, 1935–52) and in David Ayerst, *The* Manchester Guardian: *Biography of a Newspaper* (1971). Magazines have fared less well, but the student in search of information about the circulation of magazines can do worse than to start with the Madden-Dixon bibliography already cited or, for more substantive detail, with the excellent specialist introductions to each title represented in the *Wellesley Index to Victorian Periodicals* (ed. Walter E. Houghton, 4 vols., 1966–). The *Wellesley Index* contains especially helpful discussions, including circulation information, about the *North British Review* (1844–71), *Fraser's Magazine for Town and Country* (1830–82), the *Cornhill Magazine* (1860–), and the *Quarterly Review* (1809–). Among the more substantive histories of periodicals that have been written, the following contain useful information about circulation and readership: W. Beach Thomas, *The Story of the* Spectator, *1828–1928* (1928); Merle M. Bevington, *The* Saturday Review, *1855–1868: Representative Educated Opinion in Victorian England* (1941); Francis Mineka, *The Dissidence of Dissent: The* Monthly Repository *1806–1838* (1944); and Leslie Marchand, *The* Athenaeum: *A Mirror of Victorian Culture* (1941).

Advertisers' Directories

Much of the secondary literature on circulation draws heavily on another category of printed material that is of considerable importance to those interested in Victorian periodical literature: the advertisers' directories and handbooks, which were published with increasing frequency and regularity in the second half of the nineteenth century. Charles Mitchell's *Newspaper Press Directory* (known familiarly as *Mitchell's Newspaper Directory*), which commenced publication on an annual basis in 1846, is unquestionably the most valuable of the directories. Each volume includes a comprehensive listing of London and provincial newspapers, periodicals, and reviews, together with selected categories of information about each journal, including frequency of publication, price, subject of concentration, some evaluation of the political tendencies of the journal, and, occasionally, references to estimated circulation. Two other nineteenth-century directories of comparable scope are Frederick May's *London Press Dictionary and Advertiser's Handbook*, which began its annual publication in 1871 (it subsequently took the more familiar title *Willing's British and Irish Press Guide*), and Sell's *Dictionary of the World Press and Advertisers' Reference*, the first volume of which appeared in 1881. These three major press directories can usefully be supplemented by publications of a slightly different (and less illuminating) character, like the *Publishers' Circular and Booksellers' Record of British and Foreign Literature*, which dates from 1837; the *Bookseller*, which began publication in 1858; and the *Printers' Register*, which appeared for the first time in 1863.

All of the aforementioned Victorian handbooks and directories contain numerous advertisements for periodicals and newspapers as back matter in the respective volumes. By scanning these advertisements, rather than by concentrating on the official descriptive material in the front sections of the volumes (which contains relatively little detailed factual information about circulation), the student will be able to compile a considerable dossier of material on readership. Some of this information has not been replicated elsewhere. It is a largely untapped source of knowledge about distribution patterns and readership, and the consumer practices of an expanding popular market.

But caveats are in order, especially for those in search of specific circulation figures. Some of these figures may prove to be unreliable, at the very least. Beginning in the 1870s publishers' claims were occasionally reinforced by accountants' certificates, but statements inserted in directories were mostly placed there in order to lure potential advertisers and readers to journals that were seen to be "prospering." Thus the majority of the circulation claims made in the directories are little more than assertions prompted by competitive braggadocio. They cannot, in the absence of other sources, be considered as objectively valid. How many categories of "largest" or "greatest" can there be, the industrious reader is likely to ask, after scanning the back matter of *Mitchell's, Willing's,* or *Sell's*? Directories, then, are of considerable potential importance, but in the absence of objective supporting data they are apt to provide the meat for cultural speculation about the impact of print rather than the bones of statistical evidence for accurate assessments of circulation.

The Stamp Tax and the Parliamentary Returns

Where can students turn once they have exhausted the secondary literature, ingested those directories that are available (the directories mentioned are all relatively scarce outside British libraries), rummaged through the odd surviving booksellers' accounts or subscription library catalogues, and examined, however intensively, runs of Victorian journals? Is there a comprehensive printed source to which to turn for information about the readership of Victorian newspapers and periodicals? The answer, though highly qualified, is yes. The source in question—used, surprisingly, by few researchers considering its relative accessibility—is the official returns made by the Commissioners of Taxes and Stamps, in compliance with the stamp duties on newspapers and related categories of journals. These returns are scattered throughout the parliamentary papers, complete or partial holdings of which are in the possession of most libraries, either in the originals or on microfiche. Unfortunately, the collating of data from specific returns is a complex task, since no adequate guide exists. Indexes to the parliamentary papers are of limited value inasmuch as they provide only scanty information about the contents of specific returns. The Irish University Press Series of British Parliamentary Papers reprints some of the parliamentary papers relating to newspapers, including the important Report from the Select Committee on Newspaper Stamps (1851), but it is by no means complete. Appendix A to this essay is, therefore, the first attempt to organize and list inclusively the data in the stamp returns so as to facilitate access to them.

It is ironic that the newspaper duty should indirectly furnish the student of Victorian journalism with one of the best opportunities to chronicle its growth. For while the tax remained in existence it obstructed the circulation of journals to a greater extent than any other single factor. Imposed initially as a revenue measure in 1711 and not finally repealed until 1855, the tax on newspapers tended to ignite the political sensibilities of a broad spectrum of reformers. It was viewed, rightly, as an indirect form of political censorship, especially between 1815 and 1836, when it stood at the imposing level of four pence. (Its actual incidence was less since the Stamp Office allowed a twenty percent discount for partial cash payment and purchase of stamped paper in bulk.) Levied on each copy of a journal rather than on its entire edition, the stamp was the most noxious of a series of financial imposts on newspapers and periodicals that came to be referred to collectively as the "taxes on knowledge." Penalty for failure to pay the duty was the impossibly steep fine of twenty pounds per copy.

Reformers struggled to repeal these duties—which included taxes on pamphlets, advertisements, and paper—and achieved success slowly during the middle decades of the nineteenth century. The pamphlet duty (levied on the total edition of a work and not on single copies) was removed in 1833; advertisement duties were reduced substantially in 1833 and fully repealed in 1853; and the excise duty on paper was removed in 1861 after a budgetary struggle that raised important constitutional issues. But throughout these struggles the newspaper tax remained the focus of the most bitter opposition. After a six-year agitation involving considerable class rancor and led by the working-class journalists Henry Hetherington and James Watson and by the Benthamite reformers Francis Place, Joseph Hume, and John Arthur Roebuck, the newspaper tax was reduced to the marginal sum of one penny per copy in 1836. It continued, however, to be an object of acrimony, particularly among those reformers who conceived of journalism as performing a central function in the shaping of political and social values. Success was achieved at last in 1855 when the duty was repealed completely, following an effective parliamentary agitation waged by Thomas Milner-Gibson and John Bright. After 1861, therefore, no "taxes on knowledge" remained to obstruct the expansion of journalism. And these latter decades, not surprisingly, were marked by an explosion of popular journalism that saw vastly increased circulations and considerably reduced prices.

The parliamentary returns recording the payment of the stamp duty on newspapers are by no means a perfect basis for calculating circulations, and before the student proceeds to use them, their deficiencies had best be taken into account. The most persistent weakness is their limited scope. Some of the most familiar names in Victorian journalism—of newspapers as well as of magazines and reviews—are not found in any of the parliamentary returns because their owners paid no stamp duty. The returns contain no references to the *Family Herald, Chambers' Edinburgh Journal,* the *Daily Telegraph,* the *London Journal, Macmillan's Magazine,* the *Edinburgh Review, Blackwood's Edinburgh Magazine,* and numerous other journals that defined the texture of Victorian journalism.

Most magazines and reviews were exempted from payment of the tax, but the position of newspapers was ambiguous. Uncertainties were fed by successive stamp acts that redefined the extent of fiscal obligation. Originally, newspapers, i.e., journals that purveyed "public news" directly, were alone subject to the impost; other types of journals were excluded. But an act passed in 1819, intended to annihilate the cheap radical press, extended the tax to journals that contained "remarks" on news. The qualifying extension—one of considerable importance, since the boundary between "news" and "remarks" was tenuous—had to do with the frequency of publication. If a journal was published more often than once every twenty-six days—regardless of whether it conveyed news or merely commented upon it—it became subject to legal penalties. From 1819 on, therefore, monthlies and quarterlies continued to be excluded from the scope of the newspaper duty. However, some weekly and bimonthly periodicals that were previously exempted fell within the purview of the stamp tax.

Fortunately for researchers seeking data about circulation (though not for the health of Victorian journalism), the fiscal constraints were tightened beginning in 1836. Although the tax was reduced to one penny in that year, several categories of previously excluded journals became subject to the stamp duty. Papers that printed "public news," as opposed to "class news" (information that was of interest to a particular category of readers), irrespective of the frequency with which they appeared, were required to pay the tax. This meant the inclusion of many monthlies previously unaffected. However, absurd anomalies arose within the law. Both the *Legal Observer* and, more dubiously, John Cassell's innocuous penny temperance miscellany, the *Working Man's Friend,* were defined as "class news" journals and exempted from payment of the duty, Cassell's publication being allowed to function legally because the Board of Inland Revenue was eager not to harass retailers of noncontroversial and "moral" works. Yet although many similar monthlies were also informally exempted from payment of the duty, Charles Dickens' temperate *Narrative of Household Events* was threatened with prosecution for nonpayment of the duty, as were the even blander monthlies the *Norwich Reformer* and the *Freeholder,* the latter also published by Cassell. Thus after 1836 the parliamentary returns contain a significant increment of new periodicals, as is made clear by comparing the July 1835–April 1836 returns with those for the years 1837–50. The former list 79 London periodicals, while the latter record more than 625 for London. Partly this difference is a function of sheer growth; but mostly it is the result of a widening legal net, as is indicated by titles such as *Parish Choir, Peace Advocate, Water Cure Journal, Temperance Recorder, Country Gentleman,* and *Leisure Moments* in the 1837–50 returns. Yet the idiosyncratic nature of so many of these titles combined with the absence of many influential journals make the post–1836 stamp returns much less useful than might be expected. Two nineteenth-century sources that illuminate the anomalies of the stamp act during the years 1836 to 1855 are Collet D. Collet, *History of the Taxes on Knowledge: Their Origin and Repeal* (2 vols., 1899), and the multitudinous evidence presented by witnesses called before the Select Committee on Newspapers Stamps in 1851 (Parliamentary Papers, 1851, XVII).

An additional factor that affected the comprehensiveness of the stamp returns was the link between fiscal obligations and postal privileges. Proprietors of liable journals were allowed free transmission of their journals through the Post Office in exchange for payment of the stamp tax. Although an 1840 regulation reduced the benefits of this arrangement by restricting it to papers delivered outside a three-mile radius of the General Post Office in London, it was an important concession, especially for those publishers and distributors whose journals were transmitted to outlying areas of the country. The reselling of worn journals was a common practice in Victorian times, and free postal transmission greatly facilitated this, too, since journals could be forwarded several times through the post free of charge.

As railways superseded coaches in the 1840s and consumers came to give priority to speed, distribution of journals through the post became less requisite to publishing success. But some publishers—including those who printed larger and thicker editions than the norm and hence were liable for increased carrying charges—continued to regard free use of the Post Office as a handsome concession. Many of them paid the stamp duty voluntarily in order to secure this privilege, an option that was facilitated after 1836 because of the greater discretion in the law. The greater the number of publishers who paid stamp duty (from whatever motivation), the richer the harvest of statistical returns; yet frequently the value of the parliamentary returns was diminished by the very incentives that produced them. For example, the splitting of editions of a journal into stamped and unstamped copies became an increasingly common practice due to the postal concession. A portion of a journal's run would be distributed "legally" through the Post Office and recorded in the parliamentary papers on the basis of the paid stamped paper, while the remaining copies would be distributed privately so as to gain the advantages of speed and flexible deliveries. These unstamped copies, not being printed on stamped legal paper, were therefore not recorded in the parliamentary returns.

Limitations of the Stamp Returns

In 1855, when the newspaper duty was totally repealed, the practice of "splitting" editions became institutionalized. For the next fifteen years (up to 1870) publishers were given the option of paying no duty at all and making private arrangements for distribution of their journals or of paying a penny duty in exchange for postal privileges. Parliamentary returns continued to be issued during these years, but the splitting of editions became so pervasive that these returns are, at times, indecipherable. Extreme caution is required if the 1856–70 returns are to be used with any degree of accuracy. It is possible, for example, to calculate the percentage of stamped copies of a given journal's run, but only by working out formulas based on the 1854 and 1856 returns. Ellegård, in the article cited, has devised coefficients for a large number of periodicals published in the 1860s, based precisely on such an analysis. However, his conclusions are fragmentary and, more often than not, unreliable. They represent little more than suggestive hypotheses that frequently break down as soon as they are matched against more reliable figures. Furthermore, as circulations began to increase (reducing per capita distribution costs of copies of journals), it became less common for journals to stamp more than an insignificant portion of their runs. By the 1860s, therefore, the parliamentary returns are often misleading.

Even when dealing with the fullest returns, which are to be found between 1837 and 1854, there are further difficulties to be encountered. The complexities of the stamping system created problems, as the Commissioners of Taxes and Stamps themselves vociferously affirmed on several occasions. Paper had to be stamped before printing. The procedure for accomplishing this took two forms: purchasing unstamped paper from wholesalers or manufacturers and then shipping it to one of the government stamping establishments in London, Manchester, or Edinburgh; or, alternatively, negotiating the entire complex process through agents, usually based in London. Provincial publishers relied mostly on the latter alternative because the stamping establishments were not easily accessible to them. But their London counterparts often chose that method for reasons of efficiency and cost.

When the process was effected in this way it meant that the proprietor of a journal had no direct contact with the Stamp Office. Negotiating agents registered the proprietor's name at the Stamp Office, but since they settled their accounts on a monthly basis they frequently did not bother to distinguish between one journal and another, although legally required to do so. As a result, the parliamentary returns do not always distinguish between two or more papers owned by the same proprietor. The *Times* and the *Evening Mail*, published jointly up to 1854, appear as a combined entry in the pre-1837 stamp returns, as do the *True Sun* and the *Weekly True Sun*, the *Morning Herald* and the *English Chronicle*, and other groups of journals. In order to obviate some of these difficulties, the Stamp Act of 1836 required that a "distinctive die" be used by each journal (the title of the journal was to appear on the stamp), a practice that, according to the *Times*, was intended to "smoke out its circulation."

Although combined listings of journals owned by single publishers disappeared from the parliamentary returns after 1836, the requirement that a separate dye be used was not always sufficient to deter "stamp-swopping." This practice often stemmed from publishing stratagems that were deliberately obfuscatory. For commercial reasons, proprietors "borrowed" or purchased stamps from each other. Two provincial newspapers, for example, the *Manchester Times* and the *Manchester Chronicle*, deliberately overbought stamped paper so as to inflate their "official" circulation figures. Like the publishers' claims in the press directories of the period, the resulting parliamentary returns were intended to magnify the appeal of these journals to prospective subscribers and advertisers. The unused paper ("distinctive dye" and all) was then sold privately at a discount to other proprietors. According to one account, the *Manchester Chronicle* was so immersed in this competitive tactic that it sold excess stamped paper to grocers for wrapping when it could not persuade other newspaper proprietors to absorb its surplus. On at least one occasion, the *Manchester Times* displayed the *Chronicle*'s wrapping material in its shop window in order to "expose" the fraudulent maneuvers of its rival.

A less obtrusive difficulty with the stamp returns is the problem of wastage. Wastage must always be taken into account in assessing a journal's true circulation, but given the stability of nineteenth-century distribution practices (the corner news vendor and the news agent's shop were comparatively late innovations), it was not so significant a factor as it became subsequently. Nonetheless, sheets of paper stamped and paid for at the Stamp Office are not automatically convertible into numbers of sold copies. Some proprietors deliberately overpurchased stamps as a speculation in "news." If the size of an issue had to be curtailed, the extra paper could be stored for future use. The reverse practice was more common: the failure (usually inadvertent) to buy sufficient stamped paper to cope with sudden increased demand, as when "sensational" news items supervened. Sales of the *Times* or the *Observer* or the *Weekly Dispatch* might respond vigorously to well-publicized events: a war dispatch proclaiming victory over the Russians or, more simply, a lurid account of murder or rape. Proprietors would then print unstamped copies and distribute them illegally through the Post Office, paying back the sums of money owed to the government later. This practice, if not engaged in too aggressively, was overlooked, but the parliamentary returns were likely to show considerably lower circulation than actually existed, just as in the previously cited example they would give an impression of higher circulation. For these reasons monthly stamped returns (as provided between 1837 and 1843) are sometimes less useful than quarterly or annual figures, since distortions can be eliminated only by a flattening out of the returns over a longer period of time.

Notwithstanding numerous weaknesses, the Stamp Office returns are the best available evidence for determining the circulations of many Victorian newspapers and periodicals. There exists a complete run of figures from 1829 to 1870, with the unaccountable exception of 1834. These figures are of mixed quality. Before 1836 they are spotty; between 1837 and 1854 they are impressively complete and reliable; and from 1856 to 1870 they are, for the reasons indicated, hazardous to use. Parliamentary returns record the number of stamps purchased on an annual, quarterly, or monthly basis (and during 1832 to 1833, on an eighteen-month basis), and the investigator must translate these raw statistics into workable circulation figures. If frequency of publication is indicated in the return, or otherwise known, the best method is to take the annual, quarterly, or monthly stamp figures and divide them by 52, 13, or 4.25, for weeklies; by 104, 26, or 8.50, for biweeklies; and by 312, 78, or 25.5, for daily journals. This mathematical operation is likely to lead to conclusions that are inaccurate in specific detail but sufficiently illuminating to indicate general circulation trends and changing patterns of demand.

The returns are best between 1837 and 1854, when they were issued regularly on both a monthly (1837–43) and an annual basis and when the largest number of journals paid the duty. With monthly and annual returns available for part of this period, both long- and short-term trends in circulation can be pinpointed effectively. There are some discrepancies in the figures, but these are usually minor and often the result of printing errors. That the Stamp Office returns are relatively accurate for 1837–54 can be demonstrated by comparing some returns extracted from the parliamentary papers with independently reliable data. One example involves the *Times*. Mowbray Morris, who managed the

Times, testified before the Select Committee on Newspaper Stamps in 1851 that the paper's circulation was 39,000 per issue; calculations derived from the stamp returns place it at 40,100. Similarly, figures for the *Manchester Guardian* correspond to independent data within an acceptable margin of error. According to the official account books of the *Manchester Guardian* used by Ayerst in his history of the newspaper, its circulation was about 6,000 in the late 1830s and 9,000 in 1846. The Stamp Office calculations for these years (based upon raw stamp returns) work out as follows: 1839—5,800; 1840—5,900; 1846—9,600. None of these figures mesh precisely, but all are close enough to be useful. Appendix B reprints additional sample calculations from the stamp returns that are thought to reflect accurately trends in circulation.

However, from 1856 on, returns are progressively more inaccurate because of the noncompulsory structure of the system. But if employed with considerable caution, these returns may delineate changes in a journal's fortunes. A dramatic increase in a journal's use of stamped paper after 1855 (which is highly unlikely) or an equally sudden decline will, in all probability, indicate nothing more significant than abandonment or adoption of the practice of "splitting." But more modest changes in the stamp figures may indicate actual shifts in the number of readers. The quarterly figures issued during these years are better than the annual or monthly ones, since the intermediate time span most closely reflects changing market conditions rather than short-term responses to governmental policy. Students are best advised to consult Ellegård before using the returns for 1856–70, but it should be borne in mind that he is too optimistic about their usefulness.

To make sense of Victorian newspaper statistics is an ambitious undertaking, and only those thoroughly immersed in the details of journalism can weigh the usefulness of the stamp returns against more impressionistic bits of evidence gathered from other sources. Perhaps the returns can be characterized most validly as gauges of trends in journalism during several critical decades of the nineteenth century. If the journals being investigated never confronted the Commissioners of Taxes and Stamps, then the returns are utterly worthless; otherwise, they may be solid sources of revealing information. Herbert Spencer (in another context) once confided this observation to his diary: "At times, I pour before me my little hoard of facts, a tiny heap it is, some of it base coin too." It may be impossible to improve upon this as a description of the tasks facing the student of nineteenth-century periodical circulation, but greater familiarity with the stamp returns is likely, at least, to eliminate some of the "base coin."

Appendix A

A Descriptive Guide to the Contents of the Stamp Returns, 1824–70

The parliamentary papers are listed according to the method employed in the standard catalogues: session or date; the number of the paper as ordered to be printed; the volume of the collection as annually arranged; and the first page number. London, England, Scotland, and Wales are referred to as separate entries in the returns, but use of the word "complete" in this appendix means that figures from all four areas are included in the return. "Not printed" means that only the title page, not actual figures, is given.

Note: The stamp returns for Ireland are not listed in this appendix.

Year	Session	Number of Paper	Volume	Page	Description
1824	NO RETURN				
1825	1830	609	25	347	England Annual NOT PRINTED
1826	1830	609	25	347	England Annual NOT PRINTED
1827	1830	609	25	347	England Annual NOT PRINTED
1828	1830	609	25	347	England Annual NOT PRINTED
1829	1830	609	25	347	England Annual NOT PRINTED
	1830	549	25	349	London (incomplete) Annual
1830	1831–32	30	34	127	London Annual
1831	1831–32	290	34	119	London Annual
	1831–32	465	34	121	Scotland Annual
1832/33	1833	657	32	607	London Eighteen Months (Jan. 1832–June 1833)
	1833	758	32	609	London Eighteen Months (Jan. 1832–June 1833) (an amended return that includes information on frequency of publication)
	1833	569	32	613	England Annual (Apr. 1832–Mar. 1833)
1834	NO RETURN				
1835	1836	294	45	345	Complete Monthly (July-Dec.)
	1836	388	45	357	(Complete Monthly (July-Dec.) (a supplementary return with some corrected figures)

Year	Session	Number of Paper	Volume	Page	Description
1836	1839	548	30	503	Complete Annual
	1836	294	45	345	London/England Monthly (Jan.-Apr.)
1837	1851		17	524–71	Complete Annual (an appendix to the Report of the Select Committee on Newspaper Stamps, which constitutes an entire volume in the Parliamentary Papers)
	1852	42	28	497	Complete Annual
	1839	548	30	503	Complete Annual
	1837	526	39	305	Complete Monthly (Jan.-June)
	1837–38	73	36	393	Complete Monthly (July-Nov.)
	1837–38	368	36	403	Complete Monthly (Dec.)
	1837	232	39	321	London Monthly (Jan.-Mar.)
1838	1851		17	524–71	Complete Annual
	1852	42	28	497	Complete Annual
	1841	407	13	481	Complete Annual
	1839	548	30	503	Complete Annual
	1837–38	368	36	403	Complete Monthly (Jan.-Mar.)
	1839	9	30	469	Complete Monthly (Apr.-Dec.)
1839	1851		17	524–71	Complete Annual
	1841	407	13	481	Complete Annual
	1852	42	28	497	Complete Annual
	1839	213	30	483	Complete Monthly (Jan.-Mar.)
	1839	449	30	493	Complete Monthly (Apr.-June)
	1840	15	29	483	Complete Monthly (July-Dec.)
1840	1851		17	524–71	Complete Annual
	1841	407	13	481	Complete Annual
	1852	42	28	497	Complete Annual
	1840	266	29	503	Complete Monthly (Jan.-Mar.)
	1840	525	29	513	Complete Monthly (Apr.-June)
	1841	407	13	481	Complete Monthly (July-Dec.)
1841	1851		17	524–71	Complete Annual
	1852	42	28	497	Complete Annual
	1841	407	13	481	Complete Monthly (Jan.-Mar.)
	1841 (sess. 2)	26	2	45	Complete Monthly (Apr.-June)
	1842	44	26	561	Complete Monthly (July-Dec.)
1842	1851		17	524–71	Complete Annual
	1852	42	28	497	Complete Annual
	1842	257	26	587	Complete Monthly (Jan.-Mar.)
	1842	579	26	601	Complete Monthly (Apr.-June)
	1843	98	30	513	Complete Monthly (July-Dec.)
1843	1851		17	524–71	Complete Annual
	1852	42	28	497	Complete Annual
	1843	282	30	559	Complete Monthly (Jan.-Mar.)
	1843	611	30	571	Complete Monthly (Apr.-June)

Year	Session	Number of Paper	Volume	Page	Description	
	1844	55	32	419	Complete	Monthly (July-Dec.) (contains information on frequency of publication)
1844	1851		17	524–71	Complete	Annual
	1852	42	28	497	Complete	Annual
1845	1851		17	524–71	Complete	Annual
	1852	42	28	497	Complete	Annual
1846	1851		17	524–71	Complete	Annual
	1852	42	28	497	Complete	Annual
1847	1851		17	524–71	Complete	Annual
	1852	42	28	497	Complete	Annual
1848	1851		17	524–71	Complete	Annual
	1852	42	28	497	Complete	Annual
1849	1851		17	524–71	Complete	Annual
	1852	42	28	497	Complete	Annual
1850	1851		17	524–71	Complete	Annual
	1852	42	28	497	Complete	Annual
1851	1854	117	39	479	Complete	Annual
	1854	238	39	501	Complete	Quarterly
1852	1854	117	39	479	Complete	Annual
	1854	238	39	501	Complete	Quarterly
1853	1854	117	39	479	Complete	Annual
	1854	238	39	501	Complete	Quarterly
1854	1854–55	83	30	497	Complete	Annual
	1854	238	39	501	Complete	Quarterly (Jan.-Mar.)
	1854	475	39	519	Complete	Quarterly (Apr.-June)
1855	1854–55	438	30	507	Complete	Quarterly (Jan.-June)
	1857–58	489	34	259	Complete	Quarterly (July-Dec.)
1856	1857–58	489	34	259	Complete	Quarterly
1857	1857–58	489	34	259	Complete	Quarterly
1858	1859 (sess. 2)	230	15	495	Complete	Quarterly
1859	1859 (sess. 2)	230	15	495	Complete	Quarterly (Jan.-June)
	1860	151	40	621	Complete	Quarterly (July-Dec.)
1860	1860	151	40	621	Complete	Quarterly (Jan.-June)
	1861	531	34		Complete	Quarterly (July-Dec.)
1861	1861	531	34	621	Complete	Quarterly (Jan.-June)
	1862	498	30	519	Complete	Quarterly (July-Dec.)
1862	1862	498	30	519	Complete	Quarterly (Jan.-June)
	1864	27	34	29	Complete	Quarterly (July-Dec.)
1863	1864	27	34	29	Complete	Quarterly (Jan.-June)
	1865	471	31	65	Complete	Quarterly (July-Dec.)
1864	1865	471	31	65	Complete	Quarterly (Jan.-June)
	1866	491	40	113	Complete	Quarterly (July-Dec.)
1864/65	1867–68	359	55	493	Complete	Annual (July 1864–June 1865)
1865	1866	491	40	113	Complete	Quarterly

Year	Session	Number of Paper	Volume	Page	Description	
1865/66	1867–68	461	55	539	Complete	Annual (July 1865–June 1866)
1866	1866	491	40	113	Complete	Quarterly (Jan.-June)
1866/67	1867–68	461	55	539	Complete	Annual (July 1866–June 1867)
1867/8	1867–68	461	55	539	Complete	Annual (July 1867–June 1868)
1868/69	1870	248	41	385	Complete	Annual (July 1868–June 1869)
1869/70	1870	460	41	399	Complete	Annual (July 1869–June 1870)

Appendix B

Some Sample Circulations Derived from the Stamp Returns, 1829-54

This appendix lists some sample estimates of circulations of news-papers and periodicals based upon the stamp returns for the years 1829–54. The intent is to illustrate the research possibilities offered by the parliamentary papers, not to provide inclusive information. Annual figures have been used as the basis for the calculations: raw stamp returns have been divided by 52 (weeklies), 104 (biweeklies), or 312 (dailies). Returns are not included for the years 1855–70 as these figures are unreliable unless used cautiously. Students interested in these figures are advised to consult Ellegård's article. Circulations have been rounded off to the nearest hundred.

Bell's Life in London (London, weekly)

1837	16,400
1840	22,600
1845	29,200
1850	24,700
1854	22,300

Bell's New Weekly Messenger (London, weekly)

1837	4,100
1840	1,400
1845	1,300
1850	400

Birmingham Gazette (Aris') (Birmingham, weekly)

1837	3,000
1840	2,900
1845	2,100
1850	2,300
1854	2,300

Courier (London, daily)

1829	3,200
1836	1,400
1840	800

Economist (London, weekly)

1844	1,800
1850	3,800
1854	4,300

Examiner (London, weekly)

1829	5,200
1837	3,900
1840	6,000
1845	5,100
1850	4,400
1854	4,800

Glasgow Herald (Glasgow, biweekly)

1831	1,600
1836	2,400
1840	3,200
1845	3,700
1850	3,800
1854	5,200

Globe (London, daily)

1836	2,800
1840	3,200
1845	2,700
1850	1,900
1854	2,700

Manchester Guardian (Manchester, biweekly)

1837	4,700
1840	5,900
1845	9,300
1850	9,000
1854	10,300

Morning Advertiser (London, daily)

1836	4,500
1840	4,900
1845	4,600
1850	5,000
1854	7,600

Morning Chronicle (London, daily)

1837	6,200
1840	6,700

1845	5,000
1850	2,900
1854	2,800

Newcastle Courant (Newcastle, weekly)

1836	2,600
1840	3,800
1845	4,300
1850	4,800
1854	5,300

News of the World (London, weekly)

1845	24,100
1850	56,300
1854	109,100

Nonconformist (London, weekly)

1842	1,900
1845	1,700
1850	1,200

Northern Star (Leeds, London, weekly)

1838	11,000
1840	18,800
1845	6,500
1850	4,700

Punch (London, weekly)

1845	8,600
1850	6,600
1854	8,200

Satirist (London, weekly)

1836	3,700
1840	3,700
1845	1,600
1848	1,200

Scotsman (Edinburgh, biweekly)

1837	2,500
1840	2,400
1845	2,400
1850	2,900
1854	3,500

Spectator (London, weekly)

1836	2,700
1840	3,500
1845	2,600
1850	2,900
1854	2,700

Times (London, daily)

1837	9,800
1840	16,200
1845	26,000
1850	38,100
1854	51,200

Weekly Dispatch (London, weekly)

1837	50,100
1840	43,750
1845	47,250
1850	37,500
1854	38,100

Index